HEALING IN HELL

The Memoirs of a Far Eastern POW Medic

KENNETH ADAMS

Pen & Sword
MILITARY

First published in Great Britain in 2011 by
PEN & SWORD MILITARY
An imprint of
Pen & Sword Books Ltd
47 Church Street
Barnsley
South Yorkshire
S70 2AS

ISBN 978-1-84884-575-6

A CIP catalogue record for this book is
available from the British Library

Typeset by Concept, Huddersfield, West Yorkshire
Printed and bound in England by CPI UK

Pen & Sword Books Ltd incorporates the Imprints of Pen & Sword Aviation,
Pen & Sword Maritime, Pen & Sword Military, Wharncliffe Local History,
Pen & Sword Select, Pen & Sword Military Classics, Leo Cooper,
Remember When, Seaforth Publishing and Frontline Publishing

For a complete list of Pen & Sword titles please contact
PEN & SWORD BOOKS LIMITED
47 Church Street, Barnsley, South Yorkshire, S70 2AS, England
E-mail: enquiries@pen-and-sword.co.uk
Website: www.pen-and-sword.co.uk

HEALING
IN HELL

Contents

Preface

Sixty-five years is a long time to wait to tell a story about my life as a prisoner of war of the Japanese in Singapore and Thailand. During most of those years I rarely talked about it. The odd anecdote was more than enough for me and certainly for my family. I wanted to move on with my life. They wanted the same.

So why revisit it now? The principal reason is that, at ninety-one, I want to make more sense of those far-off, but not forgotten, years when, as a young medical orderly, I played a tiny part in a fight against disease and death. I want to understand better how those events influenced my post-war life while I was busy consigning them to the irrelevant past. My grandson, Richard, listened to many of my stories during his university vacations in 2005 and 2006. This started me thinking seriously about the different events and incidents described here, how they might be connected and what they mean to me. My daughter Diane and grandson Mark provided further encouragement. Finally, my son Mike's willingness to come over from Australia and spend several weeks here in early 2009 discussing my time as a Far Eastern prisoner of war and its wider social and political context provided the motivation to move ahead.

In this book I have not attempted to demonise the Japanese or congratulate a withering band of men on their survival skills. I certainly have not attempted to write a history. I have the hubris to believe I am still too young for my times to be seen as history. My memory of scenes, people, events, and conversations is clear but precise times and places of particular events are less so, in some cases because the contextual facts were unknown to me at the time. My POW experiences are also compartmentalised and restricted by the camps I went to and when I went to them.

I have attempted to do three things in my book. First, to set out personal challenges and how they were dealt with both at Changi and Kanchanaburi and during the increasingly desperate trek through eastern and central Thailand during the closing months of the war. Secondly, to explain some of the difficulties of reintegrating into post-war Britain and finally, to offer personal perspectives on such disparate issues like Japan's responsibility for all the pointless deaths in captivity from ill-treatment, malnutrition and tropical diseases, and issues like friendship and survival. If these insights are of some interest to others, that would be very satisfying to me.

The text is based on numerous discussions with Mike, Richard and Mark and, inevitably, is informal and conversational. I would like to thank Mike for taming the text and putting it into a form that can be published, and my wife Marion for her forbearance in putting up with long hours of discussion and taping on a subject that has never been among her favourites. I also would like to thank my son-in-law, John Roberts, for proofreading various drafts of this book and my daughter-in-law Pauline, who has supported the project and put up with Mike's long absences in England over the last two years.

Kenneth Adams
Burnt Yates, near Harrogate
February 2011

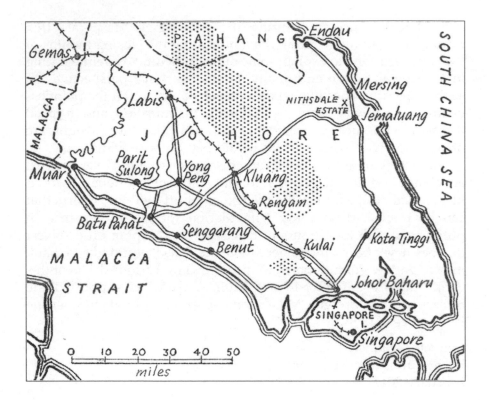

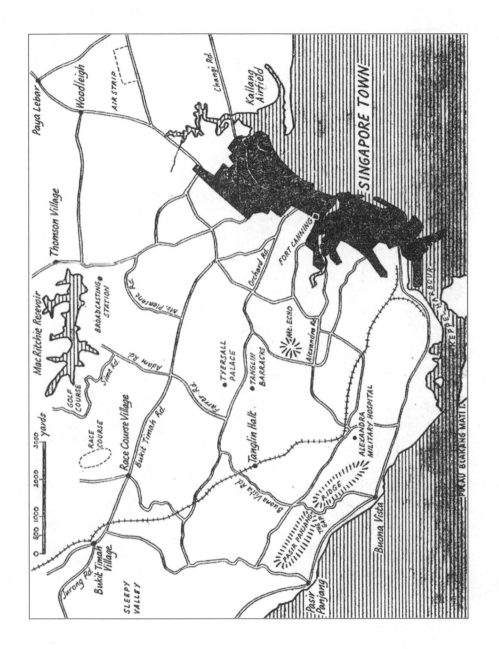

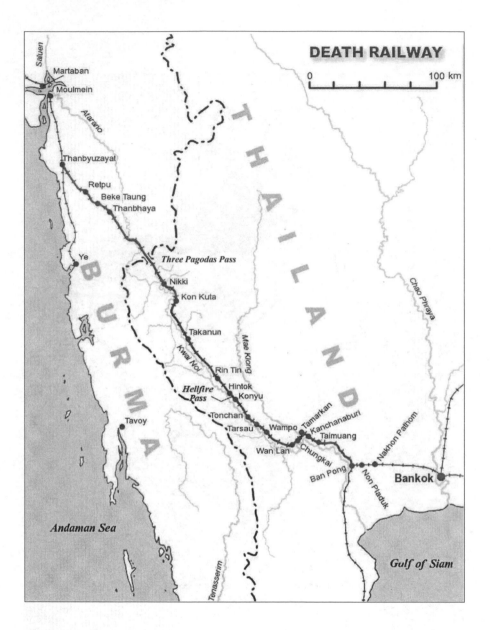

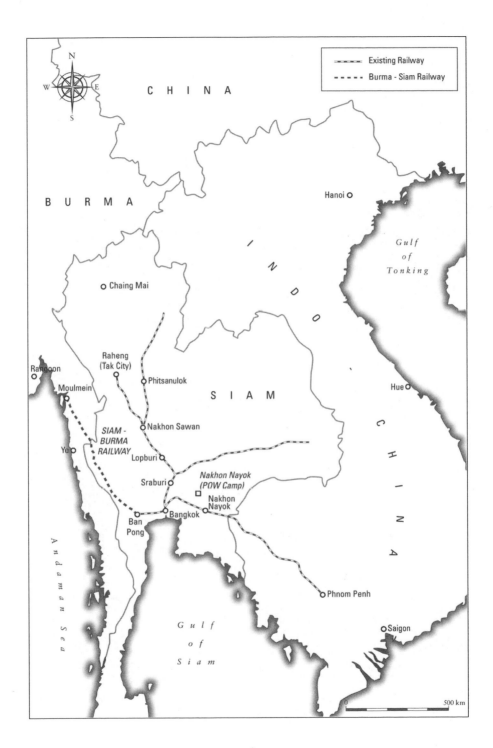

Introduction

I have never thought about writing a book – or contributing to one – about my time as a Far Eastern prisoner of war. For me it was enough to tell my stories at last to a few people who were interested in them. But when the opportunity came to transform my anecdotes about being a young medical orderly in the Royal Army Medical Corps (RAMC) into something more permanent, more organised and hopefully more insightful, it was too good to miss.

Delving into the past was exciting. I wasn't writing history. My POW experiences are too compartmentalised and restricted by the camps I went to and when I went to them to qualify as history. The timing of events also is sometimes very approximate. Days and nights merged during the fighting in Malaya and Singapore and months stretched and merged during the POW years. Rather, I was filling in holes in my personal narrative – the long ago friendships, the good and bad times, where I'd made a difference and where I hadn't, and what was fantasy and what reality. Personal discovery is important even at the age of ninety-one.

Delving into the past also was intimidating because it required confronting many emotions that remain raw. I still bridle at the 'rob all my comrades' slur levelled at medical orderlies in the RAMC. This alternative rendering of RAMC was a legacy of the Great War when medics were widely suspected of looting the personal effects of their dead and wounded comrades. This suspicion surfaced in a more limited way in my war, often in company with the view that 'conchies' – conscientious objectors – hadn't the guts to fight for King and Country so took the soft option of becoming medical orderlies instead. My rawest emotions all relate to family: my wife and I meeting as strangers after the war and the roller-coaster ride to re-establish relationships over the following years.

I was determined that this book must not just be another old soldier's musings about the fall of Singapore, a travel log of POW camps and a hasty paragraph or two about returning to England. These elements form the skeleton of the book – its structure and chronology – but to have value to me, and potentially contemporary value to others, I wanted to make my own sense of some universally important issues. In particular how we:

- respond to death when we see it for the first time;
- balance caring and callousness when disease and death starts to overwhelm us;
- manage the pain of long-term separation from family and friends;
- survive the powerlessness and endless frustration of indeterminate imprisonment;
- balance the fear and excitement of freedom when it arrives out of the blue;
- manage the changes wrought by war in ourselves and loved ones;
- re-build family relationships that may have worn thin or become ambiguous;
- find our places again in 'normal' society once it's all over; and
- rationalise the lottery of survival and the good and bad moments of wartime in shaping our lives.

In a perverse way, resettling in immediate post-war Britain was the hardest part for me of being a POW, at least for a time, and it has been the hardest thing to discuss here. In the camps there was structure, mates and a weird normalcy of sorts. Back home, everything was the same yet different. I'd changed. My family had changed. The workplace had changed. What now was normal? Where did I fit in? I think many returned servicemen were similarly perplexed, and perhaps servicemen still are returning from the world's trouble spots. Being a Far Eastern POW just made the adjustment that bit harder.

PREPARATION

Chapter 1

Going to War

My military service began at 8.00 pm on Sunday, 21 April 1940 at a former girls' school in Norwich that had been taken over by the RAMC. No one knew I was coming and no preparations had been made, which wasn't surprising for the newest private in the British Army at a time when hundreds, if not thousands, of young lads were joining the ranks every day.

I was shown to a room where several soldiers were sleeping on the floor, found a space and went to sleep. Next morning I joined the small queues forming for the toilet and a sink with a cold water tap, had breakfast and a perfunctory medical examination, which revealed that I was in excellent health, despite having been in bed with pneumonia throughout February and most of March and still feeling unwell. I was told uniforms were in short supply but they'd be issued to me within a few days; I would be billeted at the home of a local milkman; and I would be spoken to by the sergeant major the following day. Meanwhile, I shouldn't get under people's feet – there was a war on.

So much had happened to me in the months leading up to this point.

I'd met Marion – a beautiful, high-spirited star – and I, among the gallery of her admirers, was the one who married her at Methodist Bar Chapel in Harrogate.

The war started and I registered as a conscientious objector, which was an unpopular thing to do. It sat well with my mother, with her fiery commitment to Pentecostalism and social justice, and with my own half-formed and naive enthusiasm for evangelicalism and the power of divine healing. It sat less well with my wife and father-in-law, Len, an infantryman in the Great War, and with my employer, the West Yorkshire Road Car Company.

In January 1940 I told a tribunal in Leeds that I was prepared to join the Army or the other services, but wasn't prepared to kill a man in cold blood and wouldn't join the infantry. The tribunal accepted my objection to killing as true grounds for registering as a conscientious objector, and the chairman told me I'd wasted the tribunal's time because my willingness to serve should have been made crystal clear from the outset.

My beautiful daughter Diane was born.

I was called up and at 7.30 am on Monday, 22 April I was sitting in the office of the sergeant major of the 198th Field Ambulance in Norwich. The sergeant major didn't conform to anyone's stereotype: he was from the Regular Army, seemed to be a genuinely kind and decent man, and received a commission a few weeks later.

We discussed my scholarship to Harrogate Grammar School, which was a big deal in those days; what I'd done in my studies; leaving at fifteen to get a job to bolster the intermittent earnings of my father, a former coal miner from Allerton Bywater, near Castleford; and my job over the past five years as an aspiring cost accountant with the West Yorkshire Road Car Company. He said he'd have given me the job of office sergeant if I'd arrived a week earlier, but the job was taken. However, enough was said in those fifteen minutes to tag me as a clerk, and that – rather than being a medical orderly – became my major role over the next eighteen months prior to leaving Britain.

Training

If given the choice, I'd have preferred to join the 163rd Field Ambulance being formed in the northeast – there would have been a more solid core of Yorkshire lads – but had no complaints with the 198th. From the start it felt like a good unit. Most of the medical orderlies came from Norwich and other parts of East Anglia and many had been in the footwear industry. A sizeable contingent came from Yorkshire, particularly the coal mines of South Yorkshire, and I suppose we were there to make up the numbers.

Not many medics were well educated, even by the standards of the day, though three blokes had finished sixth form at grammar school. They were interested in literature and history, were concerned the RAMC might label them as 'conchies' and were desperate to transfer to the infantry. They secured rapid transfers to infantry officer training programmes.

6

Our training really began in early April when the 198th moved to the Raynham Hall estate, in Essex. We were formed into three companies: A and B Companies each had a complement of about fifty men and the HQ Company about a hundred. (I was in B Company for most of my Army service.) At first we were drilled in routines developed during the Great War. Both A and B Companies played the role of advanced dressing stations in close support of the infantry and HQ Company, the casualty clearing station: located well behind the lines, stretcher bearers exhausting themselves carrying simulated wounded over the long distances in between.

Later, as German armies drove deeper into Belgium and France, and as the manuals for static warfare were replaced by manuals for mechanised mobile warfare, our focus shifted to six-man teams with a truck containing medical equipment and an ambulance operating immediately behind the infantry. This approach was practiced over and over again in manoeuvres with the infantry, and the lessons learnt would eventually be applied to good effect in Malaya and Singapore.

Complementing this was training in first aid and the basics of nursing. I never had concentrated medical training because of my role as office clerk, but on quiet afternoons the medical officer in charge of the office, Major Gold, gave me time off to read some of his medical books.

Over time I passed the third and second class nursing orderly tests. The third class was like a first aid course, in which we learnt how to use splints and apply field dressings. The second class was more demanding and included the workings of the body, basic theory on the causes and propagation of disease, how different medicines work, and more complex aspects of using splints and applying dressings and bandages. The training wasn't anywhere near as rigorous as for a paramedic, but it went a little deeper into nursing. I wasn't eligible to take the test for first class nursing orderly because it required one year's practical experience in an operating theatre – experience I couldn't get in the Field Ambulance.

During these early months friendships formed and I warmed to the Army. Some of the blokes couldn't read and write too well and asked me to write to their girlfriends and wives. They'd give me the gist of what they wanted to say and I'd do the rest. I enjoyed doing it. I think many a girl would have been surprised by the flowery letters she received.

Between June and November 1940, our training continued in various parts of Norfolk – at Coltishall Hall, Barton Hall and Necton Hall, near King's Lynn. Much of the training involved going over the basics of operating as a field ambulance unit until they became second nature. Fear of invasion gripped everyone after the fall of France and the evacuation of Dunkirk.

The 198th was on active service throughout this period and the choice of our locations – all close to the sea and getting nearer with each move – reflected the spirit of the time to fight on the beaches, on the landing grounds and in the fields and streets. But among those prepared to bear arms there was little to fight with. Coltishall Hall, for example, was close to an aerodrome. On nights of high alert for possible German paratrooper landings, B Company patrolled its extensive grounds with an arsenal of five .303 rifles. We were a younger version of Dad's Army, additionally hamstrung by strictures imposed by the resident lady of the manor. Invasion or not, entry to the Hall was permitted only through a casement window, not through any of the doors; access was restricted to certain rooms; and boots were to be removed and plimsolls worn inside the building.

The seriousness of these months was liberally interspaced with lighter moments, though some weren't particularly 'light' at the time. We had the misfortune to be sent to Necton Hall, a great pile of a place that had been derelict for several years and was full of rats. We killed hundreds of them but more seemed to take their place. My office was near the front door – it had been a gunroom in more prosperous days – and there was a hole in the floorboards that provided passage for the rats. I slept on a large desk to get away from them and bunged up the hole with a petrol can filled with water, but the rats kept pushing it, producing their own martial drum beat. I couldn't sleep so I removed the can and let the rats roam. They rummaged everywhere and were insatiable. One day, I bought several unrationed chocolate bars for Marion. I placed them overnight in what had been a secure gun locker. Next morning, only bits of wrapping paper were left.

In November we left the rats and our unit went to Moffatt, in Scotland, for three or four months' training. We had some lectures and practical sessions on medical issues, did the occasional drill in the streets – there was no other place for it – and spent considerable time on manoeuvres with the infantry in many parts of Scotland, simulating close-up medical support under battlefield conditions. In the process we hiked across snow-covered hills, developed skills in map reading and using a compass, learnt the basics of how to approach positions without being seen, and even had courses in field cooking. It was fun. It was like being in the Boy Scouts and did wonders for our general fitness.

There was ample free time. There wasn't much office work. The unit was scattered in different billets around the small town and generally no one bothered us early in the morning. It was common to sleep in to around 9.00 am, though this changed abruptly once this laxness was discovered. Marion visited early in the New Year. She'd just stopped breast-feeding Diane and could leave her with her mother, Lill.

It was marvellous having Marion there. She stayed at a boarding house for two or three nights and I was given leave to stay with her. There wasn't much to do around the town. We just walked about and enjoyed ourselves. The town closed down at night. We didn't go to pubs in those days and the only cinema opened one night a week, which didn't coincide with her stay, so Marion came to our billet and chatted and joked with the lads. She got on very well with them.

Around February 1941, we were transferred to Tytherington Hall in Macclesfield, Cheshire. It was a dirty place and we didn't make it any cleaner. The toilets didn't work and the latrines were a good hundred yards from the back door of the cookhouse. Going down several flights of stairs and then into the park was a long way to go in the middle of the night, especially for blokes on the beer. They typically relieved themselves out of third-floor windows and, if desperate, used any army boots left lying around. A large can was brought into a small tiled room on the second floor, but it often overflowed and by this time many blokes strongly preferred the window option.

We had some lectures on nursing and did practical work; spent almost as much time learning about explosives, blowing up tree stumps and nearly ourselves; and worked on the heavily-bombed Liverpool docks. On one occasion we unloaded a partly submerged barge carrying supplies of flour when dockers stopped work because of an unexploded bomb nearby. On other occasions we helped to locate incendiaries on the roofs of dockland warehouses.

Some good things happened at Tytherington. Marion came to visit me, leaving Diane again with her mother. There was some useful medical training. But arguably the best thing for me was getting to know Captain Ian McDonald, a New Zealand doctor. I'd come to feel ashamed of being a conscientious objector, especially after the fall of France, the terrible bombing of British cities that I was now seeing at first hand, and mounting convoy losses in the North Atlantic.

There are some lines that have to be drawn in the sand, and prattling on about the sanctity of human life under the circumstances Britain was facing at that time seemed to me, more and more, to be empty nonsense. I started talking to Captain McDonald about this. He asked me if I still had strong convictions about the sanctity of human life, and I said I definitely hadn't. He also asked if I'd like to have the reference to being a conscientious objector removed from my file. I said I would. McDonald arranged it.

Once I relinquished my status as a conscientious objector, I applied to join the Royal Air Force as a rear gunner on heavy bombers. This was about the most dangerous thing I could volunteer for and I think I was trying to remove the stain – as I'd come to see it – of being a 'conchie' and prove my worth as a man. Very fortunately, the officer in charge of our unit didn't forward the application to the RAF.

In mid-September 1941 I had two weeks' embarkation leave with Marion, Diane and the in-laws in Blackpool. We all stayed at a boarding house and mostly just walked on the sands in the pleasant autumn sunshine and wandered around the town. We didn't see any shows. Perhaps there weren't any because it was the end of the season and wartime but, even if there had been, we didn't have much spare cash. Occasionally we watched lads from the RAF parading on the front. Some had clearly been in the service for a short time and it must have been difficult for them having locals and a few holidaymakers gawping at them and making comments.

During this time I had the odd conversation with Len about his Army experience in the Great War. He never talked much about it, but told me he'd been in a shell hole with five other blokes when a German plane strafed the lines. The others had all been killed and he'd been wounded in the shoulder. He said he'd lived because he'd lost his entrenching shovel a few hours earlier and taken the shovel of a dead German soldier – German shovels had longer shafts so the blade provided better protection for the head and neck. He didn't tell me much more, and certainly didn't talk about his embarkation experiences going back to France twenty-odd years earlier, but he did recall one image: moving about in bad light and treading on the putrefying corpse of a German soldier that exploded, covering him with rotten flesh.

The embarkation leave flashed by. I said goodbye to Marion and Diane at Blackpool Railway Station on Saturday, 27 September. Marion was crying. I was upset. It was very emotional because we really didn't know whether we would ever see each other again. What can you really say? It was a conversation to be got through. They boarded the train for Harrogate and I boarded one for Macclesfield. It was the last time I saw them for over four years.

I went back briefly to Tytherington Hall. Within a month we were at Greenock, in Scotland, waiting for a convoy to take us across the North Atlantic.

Voyage to Singapore
We left Greenock in late October on the small Polish ship, the MV *Sobieski*, in a convoy guarded, as far as I could see, by a couple of British destroyers, though I was told the escort included at least one cruiser. Our departure was done in secret to minimise the risk of U-boat attacks. I watched the coastline disappear and wondered about our chances of survival if the ship were attacked and sunk: winter was on us, the weather was bad and the ocean was rough.

As part of basic security we were not told our destination but it was obviously Canada as we kept heading west and, at some point, we were informed that the convoy was bound for Halifax, Nova Scotia. We could only guess at our ultimate destination. Most of us thought it would be the Middle East, which always seemed to be the assumption underpinning our training.

The voyage across the North Atlantic was terrible, with very high winds and mountainous seas that rose up so high you felt you could touch them. At one time the old ship broke down for three or four hours and wallowed alone in mountainous seas because the convoy wouldn't stop for one ship with mechanical problems. It was terrifying. We were sitting ducks and were lucky that we weren't attacked: neither was the rest of the convoy.

Conditions aboard ship were atrocious. The great majority of blokes were in the crowded hold and slept in hammocks, much as in Lord Nelson's time. They were terribly seasick. Medical staff were classified as ship's crew and were much better off. We had cabins

11

with berths that swung with the ship to minimise seasickness and generally were served better food.

We manned the ship's small hospital with its tiny operating theatre, dental surgery and general treatment room, where I spent most of my time. The bulk of the work was treating seasickness and attending to broken arms and legs. The decks and stairways were slick with rain and sea spray, the ship was tossed up and down and lurched from side to side, and it was so easy to fall over and get hurt.

There were two patients in isolation cabins on the top deck of the ship. Neither should have been on board: it was a relief to leave them in Halifax. One had a severe case of gonorrhoea and seemed to be escaping from his wife. The other had impetigoised scabies: his backside was a blistered seeping mess. Treating them was dangerous not because of the diseases they had but because there were no solid railings on the top deck – just wires strung across – and it would have been so easy to go over the side and drown. I always wore plimsolls whenever it was my turn to treat them.

We caught up with the convoy off Iceland in early November and the escort role was taken over by the US Navy. Our routine didn't change. We still worked on seasickness and broken bones and the weather was still as terrible, but it was gratifying that the escorts weren't just a handful of British ships but a large group of US Navy ships, including, I believe, an aircraft carrier. The Foreign Secretary, Lord Halifax, was still denying US involvement in the war. The fact that they were involved, at least unofficially, was a wonderful fillip and raised our spirits.

We arrived at Halifax on 7 November. It was a sight for sore eyes. Half the US Navy seemed to there, along with several large US passenger liners that had been converted into troopships. Curiously, some of troopships' portholes were open and cooks were ostentatiously twirling plucked chickens by their legs: I interpreted this as their unique welcome and an indication of future culinary delights. Adding to the pantomime, Canadian dockers signalled to us with welcoming signs and gestures, probably assuming we were Polish soldiers.

The 53rd Brigade – some 3,000 of us – transferred to the *Mount Vernon*, which took us down the east coast of North America to Trinidad and then across the South Atlantic to Cape Town, up the east coast of Africa to Mombasa, and eventually across the Indian Ocean to Singapore, after an abortive effort to reach Bombay. With

12

its beautiful ballrooms, sweeping staircases and luxury shops, the ship retained some of the style and opulence it must have had transporting pre-war elites across the Atlantic. Gold watches were on sale by the barrow load, bargains for anyone with surplus cash.

Six men were allocated to each cabin. It was cosy and rather hot because portholes remained closed once we were under way, perhaps on account of conditions in the North Atlantic but possibly, I thought, to slow the rate of sinking in the event of a successful U-boat attack. There were no hammocks. Scaffolding in each cabin supported three levels of stretched canvas on each side of the cabin and went to dizzying heights in what had formerly been the main ballroom. I suffer from vertigo and couldn't have slept up there.

After British wartime food, American food was fantastic. There was an abundance of chicken, pork and beef, all presented with appropriate sauces and huge quantities of thoughtfully cooked vegetables and interesting salads. It beggars belief that some of our senior officers complained about the food: it was too good for us, we'd get fat and the brigade's fighting quality would suffer, though they had a point because we did almost no exercise and certainly had no organised physical training because of the cramped conditions. The upshot was that British cooks replaced American cooks. That did the trick: the quality of the food plummeted because most of our cooks didn't have a clue how to prepare meals with good ingredients and the risks of getting fat and lethargic subsided.

American doctors and medics did all the medical work and we British medics, along with most of the brigade, started to change into tourists as we reached the calm tropical waters of the Caribbean and South Atlantic. We still had a few duties like taking supplies from the hold to the kitchen and cleaning the corridors from the lower to upper decks. But this didn't take long and I spent much of each day gazing at the ocean in different light and various moods, as well as watching marine and bird life.

There were concerts. The depth of talent was remarkable. Some of the singers and comedians were as good as the big-time acts but in reality worked in factories, workshops and offices in Civvy Street. A few blokes had worked on the stage professionally. Raffles were a standard pastime. One medic raffled a gold watch. Most lads put in a dollar into what turned out to be a con. Feelings ran high for a time and he was lucky not to be thrown overboard.

13

We had several days' shore leave in Cape Town. I explored the town and surrounding countryside, including climbing halfway up Table Mountain, with my friend from Harrogate Grammar School, Don Abbot. Local people were incredibly friendly and generous with their time and money. Cars queued up at the docks to take lads out for the day. On one occasion we were taken out of town to a long, white sandy beach protected by shark netting. The surf was magnificent – it was very similar to what I experienced many years later in Australia. We were invited into peoples' homes. Strangers paid for us at restaurants. It was a magical time.

We then left for Mombasa where again we had shore leave. It was somewhat of a let-down after Cape Town, but was pleasant enough with its large docks, few good streets, the pervading richness of tropical flowers – smelling something like potpourri – and the sight of immaculately dressed European ladies promenading up and down the main street in pools of shade created by their large umbrellas.

We left Mombasa in a convoy bound for Bombay but orders were changed after several days' sailing across the Indian Ocean, and the *Mount Vernon* made great speed back to Mombasa. We arrived back in time for Christmas and spent several days there over the festive season. There were huge numbers of turkeys on board but our British cooks part-cooked them, left them at room temperature for the best part of the day before finishing the cooking, and succeeded in ruining the feast. We ate sausages on Christmas Day, something the cooks were more familiar with and less likely to ruin. Later in the day I went into town with a group of friends and we had a great Christmas lunch for half a crown each.

The *Mount Vernon* joined up with another convoy leaving Mombasa. Once at sea we were informed that our destination was Singapore. It was smooth sailing for most of the way. We had one scare a day or two's sailing from Singapore when we entered an area seeded with Japanese mines. A mine almost scraped along the side of the ship and everyone was ordered to the other side. I and perhaps thousands more, prayed silently that the mine wouldn't explode. The thought of scrambling into lifeboats in shark-infested waters filled me with horror.

The 53rd Brigade arrived at Singapore on Tuesday, 13 January 1942. There'd been air raids on the docks for most of the day, and for much of the previous month, many of the raids involving waves of

14

twenty-seven bombers operating in their flying geese formation and carpet bombing the area. The docks looked badly battered. We were lucky to dock during a violent rainstorm that kept enemy planes at bay and gave us time to disembark. The raids resumed once the storm passed. The Americans were keen to leave but were stuck until the cargo was unloaded. The *Mount Vernon* wasn't hit.

Chapter 2

Malaya and Singapore

After disembarking from the *Mount Vernon*, we were taken by truck to a large camp on Singapore Island run by the Straights Settlement Volunteer Force (SSVF). Everything was well organised and worked like clockwork. We were escorted to the palm-thatched (attap) huts assigned to us, given time to relax, served a hearty meal, and then allowed to settle down for the night on mattresses, which came with sheets and white mosquito nets. This was one of the very few times I slept between sheets in the Army.

We spent the best part of three days at the camp waiting for something to happen. The heat and humidity were enervating. There were constant air raid alerts but no attacks as the Japanese concentrated their twenty-seven-plane bomber formations on the docks. We watched several dogfights between their Zeroes and our outnumbered and out classed Brewster Buffaloes. We checked and rechecked our medical equipment. I filled in time marking British and Japanese positions on the maps of one of our medical officers – Major Gold. Given the fluidity and speed of the war, my efforts couldn't have been particularly useful.

On 16 January, the 53rd Brigade, including the entire 198th Field Ambulance, was ordered to move out. For us the Malaya and Singapore campaigns were about to start.

Muar
We moved up the west coast of Malaya in a convoy of trucks and ambulances, our destination the Muar region, an area straddling the border between the Malayan states of Johor and Malacca about 100 miles north-west of Singapore. We were a tiny part of the grand strategy to stabilise the defence line in northern Johor State, await reinforcements of men, aircraft and other essential supplies and then, in the fullness of time, turn the tables on the Japanese once the odds moved in our favour.

Like so much else with this grand strategy, it was plagued with error. We travelled all day on the 16th, were not attacked despite Japanese fighters prowling about, made reasonable time, and camped at night in a rubber plantation within 20 to 30 miles of our destination. Inexplicably, plans changed overnight. The 198th was not needed after all in the Muar region because the Australian and Indian field ambulance services were coping well enough, but was needed in Singapore in the large military hospitals. The convoy turned around and returned to Singapore. Perhaps as a face-saving gesture, a group of about ten to twelve men was allowed to proceed on to Muar, though this was whittled back to six.

The group was led by Captain Ian McDonald (B Company), a very brave New Zealander and an excellent doctor, who was keen for our medical team to move up-country in close support of the infantry. McDonald was supported by Bill Graham, a regular soldier and natural leader, a first-class nursing orderly and a man who knew an enormous amount about hospitals and medicine. We all admired Bill so when he asked for volunteers to join the team there was a strong positive response. I was part of the team. Others included Joe Binns, from Bradford, Luther Taylor (a former wrestler), from Yorkshire, and a bloke called Popkins, who was our cook and came from Cambridge.

It took perhaps a couple of hours to reach the Muar region in our two ambulances and the truck that carried our medical equipment and towed a tanker containing safe drinking water. We stopped at a deserted *kampong* that had been turned into a command centre while McDonald went to find out where Brigade headquarters wanted us to go. He returned with two additional ambulances and their drivers, courtesy of the Indian Field Ambulance, and with news that we were needed further up the line. Some infantry officers told us to watch our left flank as the Japanese were starting to come through, but what could we do? We were unarmed, apart from two of our drivers, and just hoped to avoid an encounter on a lonely stretch of road. I recalled stories, true or not, of Japanese troops shooting or bayoneting prisoners or committing other atrocities. I felt quite nervous.

It was a long 10 miles but eventually, and without mishap, we reached our goal – an advanced dressing station set up by the Aussies at a rubber factory. They had occupied the manager's house so we moved into the rubber factory shed. The next few days were a

17

baptism of fire. We'd been cooped up on board ship for about three months so fitness levels were down. We hadn't acclimatised – knowledge of the tropics amounted to wearing hats and shirts, even on overcast days, to avoid being burnt. Apart from McDonald and Bill, none of us had been abroad before or seen a jungle, never mind trying to support the infantry in one. And now, as McDonald intended, we were positioned close behind the infantry.

I didn't see any Japanese. Occasionally I saw dim figures moving in the distance but who they were was unknown. The jungle and the rubber trees limited vision, so we heard the Japanese rather than saw them. There was a lot of shooting, mortaring and bombing. I was terrified and my stomach knotted up. It's a horrible feeling knowing there is someone – up a track or possibly behind you if they'd slipped through the jungle – who has a gun and wants to shoot you. It's also amazing what you hope, or imagine, might protect you as bombs drop and shock waves buffet you and there is no trench or ditch to dive into. I remember Popkins making tea sheltering under a card table while Japanese bombers knocked hell out of our positions a few hundred yards away. It's even more amazing, or stupid, that we tried to disguise our terror by affecting unconcern, even nonchalance, as we searched for shelter while this was happening.

With the Aussies we started treating a stream of wounded. Some were brought in on stretchers. Many blokes with bad wounds surprisingly walked in and some came in under their own steam with wounds that had been unattended for some time and were becoming gangrenous. I assisted in stabilising blokes – putting on dressings, giving a shot of morphine and patching them up as best we could. It was a bit like first aid on a conveyor belt. I also assigned priority cases to ambulances and recorded the drugs administered to them. Our three large ambulances each took four patients comfortably; our small ambulance took four at a pinch. When full, the ambulances dashed to a casualty clearing station and returned as fast as possible for the next run.

I wondered how I would cope seeing dead men and treating the badly wounded. I'd never seen a dead person before but, like many others, I coped. It wasn't bravery. I accepted it as calmly as I could and tried to hide my fears. The first badly wounded bloke I helped to treat had a split in the side of his head and part of his brain was hanging out, but somehow he was still breathing. The next one had an eye missing and an arm shot off. The next one had a large hole in his back. I held a pad over the wound – it was oozing blood – and could feel the sucking movement of his lungs through my fingers as he struggled for breath. I was badly dehydrated, hadn't eaten for most of the day and nearly fainted. I don't remember individual cases after that. They just kept on coming for the next few days.

There were constant air raids but we were never targeted directly, the Japanese apparently respecting the Red Cross flag on the rubber factory shed's tin roof. Our ambulances also were respected. One was in a slow moving convoy of trucks and military equipment when a Japanese fighter attacked the convoy. The pilot stopped firing ahead of the ambulance and then continued to attack the convoy. From that time on I think many of us started to trust that the Japanese would respect the flag, but trust is quickly replaced by doubt during a raid, and I dreaded when it was my turn to stay with patients lying on stretchers on the floor of the rubber shed as bombs were falling. I'd kneel down and talk reassuringly but was really trying to make myself as small a target as possible; I'd have crawled inside my steel helmet if there'd been space. I started to think that McDonald knew I was terribly scared and was picking on me to stay with the patients as a punishment. That, of course, was nonsense. He knew I was scared because he and everybody else were scared. We just pretended otherwise.

We stayed at the rubber plantation for about one week. It was good working with the Aussie medics. They were marvellous blokes. They were well trained, resolute, generous – they gave us a pig they'd liberated – and well armed, and had a policy of shooting first and asking questions later. I hated going through the jungle at night with the Japanese God knows where and trigger-happy Aussies patrolling the perimeter. One of my jobs was to settle work schedules with our two Indian ambulance drivers who slept in their concealed vehicles about a couple of hundred yards away through the jungle. With the Aussies about, I never forgot the password, and neither did anyone else.

We knew things were bad one evening when the Aussies started to pull out. We had received no orders to retreat and didn't know whether to stay or go, or where precisely to go if we went. The indecision was cut short by the arrival of the rearguard. Three infantry officers coolly took over our shed, set up maps on a table and told us to get out because we were a liability and they didn't want responsibility for our safety. Our ambulances and truck were off in a flash just as we heard the engineers blowing a bridge 100 yards or so beyond the rubber factory. •

Rengit

Our medical team joined up with newly arrived infantry from Singapore somewhere around Rengit, a small town a few miles further down the Malayan west coast. These troops hadn't seen action before and laughed at us as we jumped behind trees when Japanese Zeroes flew anywhere near, but they weren't laughing for long. We occasionally saw British planes and gave them a cheer, but they were rare and became rarer as time went on: they would duck and weave but couldn't seriously molest the Japanese.

Brigade headquarters was at a small village about 2 miles south of Rengit. Captain McDonald, Bill Graham and I met Brigadier C.L.B. Duke. He struck me as a hard man, a leader. He didn't wear a steel helmet, just his cap. He walked around with a tommy-gun. He didn't cower like the rest of us when an enemy aircraft came near. He went out and fired at it.

He ordered McDonald to take a small party to Rengit, 'where there was a bit of a battle', and leave a two-man team to set up a dressing station in the village. McDonald left with three medics and two ambulances but was cut off by Japanese patrols. There was desperate fighting in the area and it was the old story of being out-flanked by the Japanese. McDonald and the medics spent a day or more getting back to headquarters, moving through the jungle or, in places, crawling along drainage ditches at the sides of the road. The ambulances had to be abandoned.

Bill Graham and I set up a dressing station in an abandoned building, which the infantry protected with coils of barbed wire and a Bren gun post about 100 yards beyond us. We were on one side of the road leading into the village and 150–200 infantry were on the other side in some school grounds. It was very tense: small patrols were continually being sent out to probe the surrounding jungle; no fires were allowed so there was no cooking; conversations were whispered; all vehicles, except for our remaining two ambulances and truck, were ordered out; and the wounded started to come in. Casualties were heavy and came in waves. Some of the wounds were gangrenous. It was a hard three or four days.

The order was given to retreat. The Japanese hadn't arrived at the village but it was believed they'd come around our position and cut the road lower down. The infantry retreated through the jungle. Our restored medical team, now including McDonald and the others, was told to return to Singapore in the remaining ambulances and truck and trust to luck that the Japanese would respect the Red Cross if the road was cut. We took our chances and were fortunate not to encounter enemy patrols. We returned towards evening on 27 or 28 January. We stopped at the NAAFI on the Malayan side of the Johor Causeway. It was closing down and a large amount of stock was being left behind, including crates of beer, though we were still charged for one. We crossed the causeway and made for a nearby plantation that offered good cover, and slept inside the ambulances.

Next day we headed for a large, sprawling mixed camp of attap huts on the outskirts of Singapore City, where part of the 198th Field Ambulance was based. None of us had ever been there but we knew the general direction. On the way we had a substantial breakfast at a centre run by the Salvation Army. There was never any shortage of food at this stage of the war. Well satisfied we travelled on, the military police providing final directions to the camp and the rough location of our unit.

A day or two later, on 31 January, the Argyll and Sutherland Highlanders retreated across the causeway onto Singapore Island. The evacuation of Johor State was complete. A small section of the causeway was blown up, the ear-splitting explosion resounding across the island. The siege of Singapore had begun.

The Siege
Perhaps as a reward for being at the front for so long – it was barely two weeks but seemed infinitely longer – we were given twelve-hour leave passes and I explored the city bars with a group of medics. I didn't drink much in those days, and didn't drink at all before the war, and quickly got drunk. The more hardened blokes graduated from beer to whisky nicked from a local store and decided to visit the brothels on Lavender Street. A fight nearly broke out with a group of Aussies who wanted to monopolise the girls but they thankfully decided to go dancing instead.

Very much the worst for wear, we flagged down an ambulance and returned to camp. I went to bed to sleep it off but a senior officer had seen us falling about and decided to hold a parade on the rough ground outside our huts. Like the others, I paraded drunk and dishevelled in vest and shorts and boots unlaced. We started to drill. It was a shambles. The officer was angry, the sergeant major apoplectic. For my sins I was ordered to dig a drainage trench around a large tent that served as the sergeants' mess. I succeeded in digging up the tent pegs while the sergeants were having their meal.

Partly as a punishment and perhaps because of a recommendation from Captain McDonald to Captain Hugh de Wardener, a Canadian doctor who later became Professor of Medicine at London University, I became a member of a new medical team bound for Tengah Airfield in the north-west of the island supporting Australian and Indian Infantry, including some Gurkhas. The RAF had withdrawn, so there were no planes and only a solitary aircraftsman acting as caretaker. I expected to see miles of barbed wire, pillboxes and masses of infantry because the Japanese were just up the Kranji River and across the narrow Johor Strait. But there was none of this. The infantry were spread thinly across a large area because the Japanese weren't expected to attack the north-west of the island. The mangroves were supposed to make it too difficult for them. This was meant to be a quiet sector.

Tengah Airfield was shelled heavily and our dressing station, set up in some abandoned European houses on its western edge, was hit repeatedly. Shelling the dressing station had nothing to do with lack of respect for the Red Cross flag on the part of the Japanese. They probably didn't know we were there. They were simply pointing their guns at the airfield and sometimes hitting us. There were several dead and wounded Chinese civilians when we arrived, and relatives brought in more wounded later. Many had shrapnel wounds but most had broken bones caused by falling wooden beams and collapsing roofing material as their houses were shelled. We patched them up and buried the dead.

No one wants to linger digging graves when an area is being shelled, even if the shelling is some distance away: the sound goes through you; your eardrums feel like they will explode; you want to crawl away to safety. We rolled about half a dozen bodies into a long shallow trench and quickly buried them. One old Chinese man, who had died from shrapnel wounds, couldn't be squeezed in. I reluctantly dug a hole for him: it wasn't very deep or very long and his feet stuck out. For one moment I thought of chopping them off with my shovel. The thought would have been repugnant to me two or three weeks earlier but at the time it was compelling. Whether or not the old bloke had feet didn't make much difference to him but being back under cover made a big difference to me. I raised the shovel and was suddenly aware that de Wardener was looking at me. He didn't say a word, just moved his head from side to side. That was enough. I didn't have time to dig a proper grave but made sure the feet were covered with a mound of soil. The next heavy rains would wash it away but I hoped somebody would find him when the civilian population returned and put him right. It would have profited them to do so. We buried the old bloke with his wallet containing several hundred Malay dollars, which probably represented the hard-earned savings of an entire family.

Heavy shelling around the dressing station continued intermittently for two or three days and we were ordered to relocate to an abandoned fruit juice factory just north-east of the airfield, about half a dozen miles as the crow flies west of the causeway. The new location was pleasant. On the downside, shelling intensified over the week. The Japanese were obviously bringing up more heavy weapons, our side was returning fire and the exchanges continued intermittently day and night. But on the upside, few shells were fired in our direction and none landed close by.

We had to deal with surprisingly few casualties, military or civilian. We had time to sunbathe. We restored weary muscles soaking in an old bath tub filled with hot spring water that bubbled from a pipe near the fruit juice factory. We relaxed in a grove of shady trees on a settee and easy chairs removed from one of the houses on the other side of the airfield. We entertained blokes who dropped by with fruit juices and tea. We also had the reassurance of deep trenches – so different from the shallow, hastily dug slit trenches that served in Malaya – for those occasions when Japanese shelling strayed in our general direction.

In this almost bucolic environment and on the eve of the Japanese invasion, I had no sense of foreboding that Singapore was about to fall or that I would soon become a prisoner of war. Like so many others, I sheltered behind the myths of empire. So what if we'd withdrawn from Malaya? Singapore was an impregnable bastion. We had abundant food, water (two reservoirs brimming full with the stuff) and medical supplies, and the resources of a huge military complex. The Japanese would exhaust themselves on its defences.

Their luck would run out. How could, I still believed, short near-sighted Asians prevail over the British and people of British stock? An inspired counter-attack would hurl them back up Malaya. Something would be pulled out of the hat.

In the retreat from Malaya I'd asked some Argyles if the Japanese could be held. They were confident the Japanese could be held if they had clear operational space instead of jungle and rubber trees. For the first time, the Argyles and the rest of the infantry had a clear front. In my naivety I thought the next few months would be un-comfortable but survivable – a re-run of Tobruk or, at worst, a Dunkirk-like evacuation in many months time. I had no under-standing of how badly Singapore was prepared for a siege or of the implications of Japan's overwhelming dominance of the air and at sea after the sinking of the *Prince of Wales* and *Repulse*.

On 8 February the Japanese opened up with all the heavy weapons they had. There was bombing and shelling and then mortaring on a vast scale. It was pandemonium. The invasion was launched late in the evening through the mangroves west of the causeway. Tengah Airfield was directly in its path. A huge volume of fire was concentrated in our general direction, and some Japanese shells whistled overhead, but the great bulk was aimed at targets well away from us. I remember this interminable night for the ferocious noise and the fear produced by machine-gun and rifle fire to the north and west of us. Fighting was going on but we had no idea on what scale. We certainly didn't know it was full-scale invasion. No casualties came through that night. None of us slept.

On the morning of 9 February we were in a high state of nervous-ness when two infantry officers rushed out of a battered staff car and told Captain de Wardener that the Japanese were on the fringes of the airfield and that we must pull out fast as it might be overrun. In half an hour our two ambulances and truck were packed and on the road, and we fell back to a dressing station set up by Captain McDonald and Bill Graham in what incongruously looked like an oversized cricket pavilion set in its own grounds. I have no idea where it was precisely, except that we travelled east, away from the encroaching Japanese. We made good time: the roads weren't clogged with traffic or overly hazardous with bomb craters or broken-down vehicles, and Japanese planes didn't menace us.

McDonald and his team were treating several wounded soldiers and more were coming in. There was a great deal of work to do and three of his medical staff were traumatised. Two were corporals who walked around with paper and pencil in hand laboriously extracting names and unit details from incoming wounded, one even scribbling down the obscenities that sometimes greeted their enquiries. De Wardener agreed to reassign me to McDonald's team to help clear the wounded. He and his team, now including the traumatised soldiers, returned to camp on the outskirts of the city.

Clearing the wounded took several hours. Our ambulance drivers ran the gauntlet of getting patients to the main hospitals and then returning as fast as possible to the dressing station. The system worked well because the drivers knew the station's precise location and alternative routes as conditions changed. Wounded men flooded in at night – the peak period. They were stabilised and then moved on by ambulance. The stoicism of the badly wounded always impressed me: they were either very brave or very traumatised, or both. I treated one Gurkha who'd fallen off a building and smashed an arm in several places. Splinting it properly required two medics, but everyone was doing their own urgent work. My clumsy work must have hurt the fellow terribly but he didn't make a sound or even show pain on his face. It was remarkable.

Everyone worked around the clock doing their best in near impossible circumstances. The wounded kept coming and the queues of blokes needing urgent attention lengthened. The days stretched on and on. I subsisted on hot sweet tea, hard biscuits, butter, and marmalade.

At some time on the afternoon of 10 February, the area around the dressing station came under an intense pounding and we were forced to leave in our remaining ambulance – the drivers of our other ambulance and truck were out on jobs at this time and had no idea where we'd gone to. We moved backwards and forwards, half the time not knowing where we were and at times not knowing where the front was. We treated the wounded wherever there was temporary protection behind what we thought was the front. Sometimes, we stayed for what seemed like a long time. Other times we set up and dismantled almost immediately as retreating soldiers told us we were now the front and risked being overrun or cut off.

This happened to us at a dressing station in a rubber factory north of Thomson Village, a strategically important point guarding the northern approaches to Singapore City and close to the vital reservoirs (MacRitchie to the west and Pierce to the north), and the

Woodleigh pumping station. There were large squares of rubber lying around and I wondered if they'd cushion bomb blasts. I never found out. The road outside the factory became clogged on both sides by long lines of retreating infantry interspersed with trundling Bren gun carriers. We were told to get out.

McDonald acquired a large staff car – like a general's car – which had been abandoned, presumably because it looked important and might attract unwanted attention. In convoy with the ambulance, we retreated to Thomson Village, where the 53rd Brigade was setting up a perimeter defence, and headed for a point further south where Brigade headquarters was thought to be.

I was standing on the staff car's running board watching for enemy planes. One had just attacked, emptying the road as troops ran for cover in the drainage ditches. The pilot completed his run, saw us and circled back to attack, no doubt thinking he was about to bag a senior commander. McDonald insisted we went on, instructing the driver, Ginger, to drive like the devil was after him. Ginger needed no urging. He sped on. I clung to the running board like a limpet to a rock. The Zero lined up to attack. I wanted to leap off but the car was going too fast. The plane screamed into a dive, its machine-gun bullets ripping up the road behind us, but the dive, thank God, was ill-judged. At the critical moment the plane was too low and had to climb and circle back. That saved us. We arrived at Brigade headquarters just as the plane was lining up for its second attack on us. I leapt off the running board searching for a tree to get behind but there were blokes behind every decent sized tree. In my desperation I found a sapling and hoped fervently it might deflect a bullet.

McDonald didn't find the brigadier and was told he might be at Thomson Village. We travelled back up the road in the same staff car. The brigadier wasn't there either but someone thought he might be in a forward observation position, so McDonald decided to go half a mile further up the road. The road was very quiet and we had it to ourselves. Suddenly, a motorbike dispatch rider, bent over his machine, came hurtling around a bend. He stopped a bit lower down from us, looked surprised at the staff car and had a hurried conversation with McDonald, who jumped on the pillion seat and waved us to follow.

It seemed to take an age for Ginger to turn the big car around. The ditches limited the turning circle, there were odd noises coming from the surrounding marshland, gears were fumbled, and slowly the great car completed the turn, gathered speed and hurtled back down the road. At Thomson Village, the dispatch rider told us the Japanese were just a few hundred yards further up the road. He'd ridden through a group of them and was lucky to be alive but most were coming through the swamp, hence the sounds we'd heard.

McDonald never found the brigadier. We had no new orders and returned utterly exhausted to camp. We stayed there for perhaps a day doing nothing in particular, though someone had the bright idea to uproot some large concrete paving stones and place them around our hut between the packed earth floor and the top of our sleeping platforms – a height of about 3 feet. This foresight proved sound a few hours later when, in darkness, a Japanese patrol moved into a cemetery adjacent to the camp and opened up with a machine-gun, firing incendiary rounds and setting some huts ablaze. I could hear the rounds smashing into the paving stones and see them whizzing overhead. One officer crawled over to us and ordered us to put out the fires. He received a predictable response.

As the attack was waning an order was given to pull out. It was a terrible journey. It was in the middle of the night. There was still gunfire. The air vibrated with the scream and crashing of bombs, fortunately some distance from us. Huge fires lit up the night sky. Our Royal Army Service Corps driver panicked and couldn't get the truck to move and was pushed out of the way by a medic who'd been a truck driver in Civvy Street. Tempers flared. One of our medical officers, Captain Gotla, was in the staff car immediately behind our stalled truck. He was a wonderful man with a calm disposition, but not on that night. 'Get out and push like fucking elephants,' he cried; and we did. We didn't know where we were going and didn't much care as long as it was it was away from the camp.

Progress was painfully slow as our convoy negotiated its way through the tank traps. Journey's end was a Chinese hospital, our last position prior to the surrender. The hospital may have been the Tan Tock Seng Hospital. Whatever its identity, it wasn't too far from our beleaguered camp, had been abandoned but had been brought back into service: there were doctors and surgeons, medics, patients, and administrators organising food and medical supplies. The hospital lacked for nothing, except water.

We took it in turns to sleep. Two friends, Bill Graham and Nobby Clarke, thought they'd found a ward full of sleeping men, saw two unoccupied beds, crept in, and settled down for a couple of hours' rest. Morning revealed they'd been sleeping in a ward full of dead Chinese. Morning also revealed that the hospital was extensively damaged by bombing and shelling. The numerous shell holes in the hospital's grounds clearly explained why it had been abandoned.

The area around the hospital was shelled repeatedly over the next day or so and was dive-bombed once. We dealt with a continuous stream of wounded. From time to time medical teams took ambulances into still contested areas on the fringe of the city to bring out more wounded. In places it was impossible to know who controlled the roads and our security hinged on respect for the Red Cross emblem on the ambulance. We were never attacked, but it was frightening. I went with McDonald, who remained cool, calm and in command. I made a show of being cool and calm but was so scared I could hardly speak at times.

Many of the wounded were in a very bad state and several died. One bloke being taken for burial in the hospital grounds rose up from a stretcher and asked for a drink of water. Checks had been done in the little time that was available. A doctor had pronounced him dead and he did die almost immediately afterwards. But his temporary 'resurrection' produced a wave of alarm that went through the little assembly and especially affected one of the lads in the burial party who'd been badly traumatised.

Three or four medics were killed at the hospital. They were part of a burial party that had just returned to the hospital for lunch and had the bad luck to be at the point of impact of a shell. They were obliterated. In their place, moments later, a wooden towel rack came dancing down the ward: amazingly, it didn't fall over as it skipped along. The explosion occurred not far from a ward full of patients that I was looking after. They were sitting up in bed having their lunch, their heads moving in unison as first Japanese shells went over into our lines and then British shells went over into the Japanese lines. Watching them was like watching slow motion tennis. In a moment this dull placidity was transformed into chaos. Windows were blown out and walls flattened or holed, and shrapnel tore through a solid wooden wall, peppering patients' backs.

By some miracle none were killed – the wall must have absorbed some of the explosive force – but many were in a terrible mess. I was among the lucky ones. I was at the end of the ward furthest from the blast, heard the incoming shell and dived onto the concrete floor, grabbing a pillow on the way down. I don't know how long it took for me and the doctors and other medics to get up. It could have been a minute or more or just a few seconds. But I do know I was trembling all over when I did get up and was straining to hear the sound of any other incoming shell above the noise now being made by highly agitated patients. We dashed around trying to identify the worst cases but it was difficult to identify superficial from more serious wounds because there was so much blood. Identification methods weren't scientific. Those judged to be critically or seriously injured were placed on stretchers and carried to the operating theatre, which was already working overtime. When that was done we started mopping up the blood and removing bits of shrapnel from the other patients.

The next day was Black Sunday, 15 February, the day of the surrender.

Surrender
Like everybody else, I'd heard the rumours of imminent surrender that had been circulating since the Japanese started to consolidate their hold on Singapore Island. On Sunday morning, the rumours were much more definitive: we would surrender later that day. For once they were right, but it still came as an awful shock when finally we knew that General Percival would surrender unconditionally at 4.00 pm, though in my case, and perhaps in others, that immediate reaction turned almost instantly to one of relief that the noise – the cacophony of explosions near and far, the whine of dive-bombers, the blasting of anti-aircraft guns, the sputter of machine-guns – would stop.

The silence, when it came, was wonderful. 'Thank God I've made it' just about sums up my feelings and the feelings of my friends. In those wonderful moments, the recent past vanished; we were still unaware of the massacre of colleagues and patients at the Alexandra Hospital; the future didn't exist. Silence and safety were enough. I had my first decent sleep in weeks. The tension seeped away.

Next day, and in the days that followed, relief turned to fear and bewilderment as we started to consider the implications of the catastrophic defeat. We accepted our duty as medics to stay with the sick and wounded. We were busy at the Chinese hospital. We started to prepare for a period of great uncertainty.

The realisation that I was a prisoner of war struck me forcefully for the first time on 17 February when a small party of Japanese, led by a *gunso* (sergeant), came to take us from the hospital. (The Japanese high command decided apparently to keep their main forces outside the city on the 16th, deploying only detachments of military police to secure significant buildings.) Our guards were surly little monsters grunting, growling and kicking blokes or hurrying them along with their rifle butts. That image brought home to me that we were no longer proud British soldiers, lords of all we surveyed, but the flotsam and jetsam of a defeated army.

We had a few minutes to collect our things: we didn't have kitbags, just backpacks and side packs, so couldn't take much. I took two shirts, two pairs of shorts, socks, vests, and a good second pair of boots plus bits and pieces such as shaving equipment, soap, cutlery, a mess tin, a large medical water bottle for patients, a personal water bottle, a large (and heavy) mosquito net 'borrowed' from the Chinese hospital, and some food. A skeleton staff remained to care for patients and organise their transfer to Changi (as it turned out) in the hospital's fleet of ambulances and trucks. Less openly, they organised transfers of food, medicines and essential medical equipment.

We, in the marching party, had no idea where we were bound. We speculated it might be Malaya. I saw a handful of Japanese officers on the way: they were beautifully turned out in immaculate uniforms, highly polished boots and with hands forward so their swords didn't trail on the ground. There were numerous *gunsos*, also well dressed. The other ranks looked like they always did – travel-worn and scruffy. We didn't dare give them any abuse, fearing we'd be shot. There were no signs of real hostility; though it was clear the Japanese regarded us as failed and dishonoured soldiers who hadn't the courage to fight on when we had the numerical advantage.

The march to Changi revealed the catastrophe that had overwhelmed Singapore. The place was a shambles. There were collapsed buildings, smouldering ruins, roads blocked with masonry, tangled masses of electricity cables, and smashed vehicles. In some areas bodies from the recent fighting still littered the streets: some were badly burnt; some shapeless, sticky messes covered with flies; some bloated and rotten and starting to smell badly. I remember passing one burnt-out car: the driver had been on fire and was lying in the road 'peering' out through a faceless head – the face had literally melted away. At another point, a man was slumped over a fence, black, bloated and smelling in the tropical heat. I thought he must have been a Sikh from the remnants of his long hair and beard, but couldn't be sure. In some places, you smelt rather than saw the carnage and knew there were unburied bodies close by. The smell of decomposition and corruption was atrocious.

These horrible sights and smells contrasted with some residential areas that were substantially intact and where the 'Rising Sun' flew from many houses. I marched next to a corporal from the Cambridgeshire Regiment. He was annoyed that so many houses flew the Rising Sun and started shouting abuse at no one in particular. But who could blame the locals? They obviously thought that flying the flag was the safest thing to do. They didn't want to be beaten up or shot.

Quite a few Chinese watched us march past. They displayed neither support nor opposition as they witnessed the remaking of history. There was mostly silence. The Chinese had no love for the Japanese after what had happened to their homeland and had every reason to fear what would happen next.

I felt a curious mixture of shame, embarrassment, anger and relief as we marched along. How could the British Army suffer such a humiliating defeat? I don't know how the other blokes felt. Most didn't talk much about profound feelings and I didn't either. Being a medic I couldn't grumble at the men who'd done the fighting. They'd fought very well and I was proud that so many of them came up to us medics and thanked us for the close support we'd given them during the fighting. It was particularly gratifying when one or two said they'd believed the 'rob all my comrades' rubbish about medics being gutless, robbing bastards, but now knew it to be false. I was bitter about the senior people who hadn't developed a coherent strategy for taking on the Japanese and who, seemingly, were always outmanoeuvred by them. But in all honesty, our leaders probably didn't have the resources to do better, though this never occurred to me at the time and didn't lighten my sense of shame and anger.

31

PRISONER

Chapter 3

Changi Hospital

The overnight transformation from being members of a belea-guered, but still powerful, army to becoming prisoners of war put an enormous strain on everyone. We were now totally isolated, at the beck and call of a ruthless enemy and had no idea what might happen next. I was fearful that events might spin out of control either through misunderstanding or shear bloody-mindedness and the Japanese might end up killing us. More optimistically, I talked endlessly with friends about how long we might remain prisoners. There was nothing, apart from wild rumours, to guide us. Our officers were as much in the dark as we were, and the Japanese initially offered no clues: they seemed unprepared to take on the burden of so many prisoners, presumably because they hadn't expected to defeat us so easily or quickly.

My fears of mass slaughter only disappeared once the Japanese started to organise food supplies in late February and set teams to work in March erecting the barbed wire fences of our prisons. That fear was then replaced by the discovery that the Imperial Japanese Army believed it owned us lock, stock and barrel – not only our uniforms, watches, rings and other valuables but also our bodies, to be used and disposed of as it thought fit.

The first weeks
White prisoners were dumped at camps that sprawled across Changi in the south-east of Singapore Island: British troops were assigned to Roberts Barracks (part of which became the hospital) and Kitchener Barracks; the Aussies went to Selarang and the Dutch to India Barracks. Indian troops – about half the total – went to camps in the Nee Soon area in the north of the island. We were a tribe of strays left to fend for ourselves using the little food and equipment we'd brought with us; the much larger quantities of

food, equipment and medicines brought in by truck and ambulance in the immediate aftermath of moving to Changi; and the cases of tinned food that continued to drop off the backs of trucks driven by our blokes. For the most part, what came into Changi was inventively purloined; it didn't come from the Japanese. I didn't see a Japanese soldier at this time until one of their generals and his staff came to review the spoils of war and we were required to line the route.

We set about the urgent tasks of attending to the sick and wounded, organising food supplies, digging latrines, and clearing up the debris. Patients were housed initially wherever there was reasonable shelter. We built shelters for ourselves from bits of wood and cladding that we found scattered about, sleeping as best we could.

After a few days, the 198th Field Ambulance set up a 'hospital' at Changi Post Office and we used part of it as a billet. The building was undamaged, had toilets, washstands and clean polished floors, and was more than adequate for our few dysentery patients. Some were badly dehydrated, but there was nothing too serious because the blokes were generally quite fit. We also had a handful of infectious patients who were housed in large garage-like spaces a bit lower down from the post office. The garages were clean and dry, had concrete floors and made good small wards. I worked on them with Captain de Wardener.

Everything at the post office and garages was superficially normal but this was deceptive. Like other camps in the Changi area and elsewhere, we couldn't use the toilets because the sewers had been fractured and destroyed, and there was little or no running water because the pipes from the reservoirs had been so badly damaged. Digging latrines and carting fresh water was the hard part of these first few weeks.

Unlike the surgical teams who toiled with the hundreds of men injured in the fighting, our medical duties were not initially onerous and we had ample time at the end of each shift to settle into new accommodation, go swimming and talk to friends about rescue and being free. Freedom soon became an obsession. One of the blokes had a record player and one record – Judy Garland's *Over the Rainbow* – which he played every day. Lyrics like 'Somewhere over the rainbow skies are blue' and 'The dreams that you dare to dream really do come true', and 'Wishing upon a star' and being transported to places 'Where troubles melt like lemon drops away above the chimney tops' captured our mood, though after a while the song grated on many people's nerves.

In the first week or so, we started swimming after work at a beach near Changi. There was no wire to stop us. One day, we found dozens of dead Chinese who'd been machine-gunned or bayoneted. There was blood everywhere. We didn't count the bodies and never went back to the beach.

After the war, I found out that the killings were part of a wider Japanese purge of Singapore's (and Malaya's) Chinese community that swept up many thousands of people. The purge was a response to Chinese resistance to the invasion of Singapore – several hundred Chinese irregulars opposed the invasion as part of Dalforce – and was intended to send a strong message that Japan wouldn't tolerate opposition such as it was experiencing in China itself. For a few days, the beach incident fuelled my paranoia that the Japanese might have something similar in store for us because, by this time, we had pieced together much of the tragedy that had befallen the Alexandra Hospital on 14–15 February.

It was soon apparent that there were many missing medics and patients, and then a medic from the Alexandra Hospital, who'd escaped from the hospital through the drainage ditches, told us the story as far as he knew it. He said Indian troops had fired on the Japanese from the hospital's verandas. Japanese troops had returned fire and entered the building around midday on 14 February, bayoneting or shooting staff and patients, including one anaesthetised patient who was undergoing an operation. About fifty of our soldiers were killed.

Then the Japanese herded many dozens of hospital staff and patients into sheds on the night of 14 February, giving them no food or water. Later we found out that some had suffocated in these black holes and around 200 men were then slaughtered early on the morning of 15 February. In all, perhaps one quarter of the hospital's staff and patients were massacred.

Many of the dead were from the 198th Field Ambulance, dispatched to the Alexandra Hospital after they returned prematurely from Muar. Whether true or not, I've always understood the 198th has the dubious distinction of sustaining the biggest proportional battle losses of any unit in the British Army during the Second

World War, largely on account of this massacre. I knew some of the blokes who were killed. Most were from the HQ Company. One lad had been a comedian before the war – not a top biller but supported big acts like Stanley Holloway. He'd organised theatre digs for my wife and I while I was training at Macclesfield. Another was from the Salvation Army. He was proud and tall, open and keen to engage with people and didn't conform to anyone's crude stereotype of the dogmatic 'God Squad'.

There were rumours that the Japanese incinerated the bodies in burning oil tanks. This may be true but it baffles me how anyone could have manoeuvred close enough to those raging infernos to do anything. Whatever the disposal method, the bodies were never found.

By the end of February and early March 1942, the Japanese were satisfied with security at Roberts Barracks. Its perimeter was barb-wired so we couldn't get out, and part was transformed from a regular barracks into a hospital. Chaos still reigned with patients arriving before facilities were ready but essentially we had good quality concrete barrack blocks, three stories high, that made excellent wards – surgical, dysentery, malaria, mixed diseases; specialist units like radiology, microbiology and pharmacy; accommodation for medical staff; and a medical headquarters. The makeshift days were over, for now.

Dysentery

I was assigned to one of the dysentery wards working under the supervision of my friend and mentor Bill Graham. Dysentery and malaria patients were allocated to the Field Ambulance by default. The surgical units generally needed highly skilled nursing orderlies who normally came from the Regular Army, were fully qualified and knew their stuff. We were mostly inexperienced and had to learn about tropical diseases by observation and practice and from guidance by the doctors: tropical medicine was a standard component of British medical training given the needs of the Empire at the time. Frankly, the basics of nursing dysentery and malaria patients are much simpler than treating gunshot and shrapnel wounds.

Almost from the start, dysentery was a problem at Changi and affected nearly everyone to some extent at one time or another. This was part of a much wider problem. Dysentery swept across

Singapore in the wake of the recent fighting as damaged and broken infrastructure allowed raw sewage to contaminate the city's water supply. The outbreak at Changi may have been more serious than in the general population given massive overcrowding in the camps. Nearly 50,000 prisoners were packed into the Changi complex in the early days. I think the barracks had been built to accommodate a tenth of that number. Personal hygiene standards were often rudimentary, a fact that was difficult to change even when blokes started to die. And the Japanese placed a low priority on fixing water and sewage systems.

There was a steady stream of dysentery patients, some becoming permanent. The disease eventually overwhelmed us in the first three or four months of captivity. My first ward at Roberts Hospital had six rows of beds and many beds in each row: there were two rows down the middle of the ward, one down each side and one on each of the verandas. There were hundreds of patients – some desperately ill – who were so crowded together it was difficult to move between them, especially at night with the limited lighting. I never counted all the patients. It would have been too traumatic.

The pressure eased by mid-1942, reflecting less overcrowding and therefore conditions slightly less conducive to spreading disease. About this time, substantial numbers of POWs were moving to other camps in the Singapore area to work on the docks and various construction projects. We also were starting the fateful move to Thailand and Burma to work on the railway. When my unit moved to the second dysentery ward at Roberts Hospital in April or early May, Changi's prisoner population had fallen to about 30,000 and was soon to fall much further. We no longer had to put patients on verandas, which must have been a relief for them. It certainly was for orderlies: keeping large numbers of patients dry when it was raining and blustery was hard work. We kept patients longer to make their recovery more secure. We also felt under less pressure because our routines were better developed, more wards had been opened and there were more orderlies (though I can't remember being assisted by volunteers from the infantry and elsewhere like we were at the Kanchanaburi Hospital Camp).

The work remained intense and orderlies worked twelve-hour shifts, often returning to the ward at other times to help out or chat with patients. Patients' temperatures and pulses had to be taken and medicines dispensed. There was the never-ending drudgery of cleaning and washing. Blokes were constantly running to the latrine halfway down the hill where they watched the world and the world watched them. Some blokes, of course, couldn't make it and had to be helped with bedpans or assisted onto commodes (a grandiose name for a bamboo box and metal bucket). Some inevitably messed themselves and had to be cleaned up. Cleaning them, giving the very sick regular bed baths and keeping the ward clean were demanding tasks given the numbers involved, and were critical for retaining morale and slowing the spread of disease.

At the beginning of a shift the worst task was carrying water to the wards up three flights of stairs. At the end of a shift the worst was humping containers, bigger than dustbins, brimming with excrement to nearby cesspits. It took two of us and the stench was abominable. You had to move so carefully because you didn't want the muck spilling on you and increasing your risk of getting disease. Access to safe tap water and flushing toilets would have been a blessing. I think the water supply at Changi wasn't fixed until around October, but that was towards the end of my time there.

The basics of being an orderly in a dysentery ward came down to developing and refining the routines and organisation for managing filth. Once they'd been mastered, there was the reward of graduating from 'bed pan orderlies' to learning the good stuff – recognising the different stages in the evolution of bacillary and amoebic dysentery; understanding what you could do and when you needed a doctor's intervention; and knowing how to care for the nucleus of very sick patients. You leant how to feed them if they were on solids, how to get fluid into them and how to keep up their spirits. The pastoral side of nursing was in many ways the most rewarding.

Most dysentery patients contracted mild forms of the disease. Blokes were thin and their faces were drawn; they were evacuating a great amount and we were giving them Epsom salts – a laxative – which made them worse, but they recovered fairly quickly. Some forms of dysentery were fierce and could kill in a couple of weeks. Other forms acted over a long period of time, were equally dangerous and often killed. Bad cases left men just skin and bone. It was amazing that they could walk, as all their muscle mass had atrophied. Their skin turned pale yellow and they stared vacantly into space. In my eight months or so at Changi, 200–300 blokes died from dysentery. This was roughly one half of total deaths.

I couldn't stand seeing blokes die alone. Spending time talking to blokes, holding their hands and offering meagre reassurances didn't change outcomes in the vast majority of cases. Those who died were best out of it. They were so thin and hadn't a cat in hell's chance of getting better with the food and medical supplies we had. They'd often slip into a coma before dying. You could tell they were dying by their breathing. Their mouths would be open and their breathing became laboured. It might take a day or two for them to die.

In a small minority of cases, I think pastoral care did change outcomes for blokes hovering on the borderline of life and death. I remember nursing a bloke called Fry who was very ill and certain he was dying. Over several days I convinced him he would live. A year or so later at the Kanchanaburi Hospital Camp, I was delighted when Fry, now restored to health and fitness and driving for the Japanese, sought me out, hugged me and told me I'd saved his life. Such moments were few and very precious.

As a group of doctors and medics we experimented with various ways to ease the final days of patients. We couldn't block out the Last Post blown at burials from a hill across the valley. It's not a reassuring sound and it was heard too often, almost every day and sometimes several times a day. Patients listened in silence, some realising that their time was short and the Last Post would soon be blown for them.

We decided to screen off blokes who were fading fast. The intention was good. Deaths in the ward produced a sombre mood. Everyone looked at the dead man. It was impossible not to, particularly if he'd died in the middle of the ward. No one spoke as we orderlies pulled and shoved and hefted him onto a stretcher, and the sounds, and perhaps sights, were noticeable as we parcelled up the bloke, blocking up his passages to prevent drainage, tying up the jaw to prevent it flapping open, and wrapping him up in sacking or whatever we had. Everyone wondered who'd be next. The sickest would look more fearful than ever, no doubt thinking: I'm ill; I'm like the dead bloke was; am I next?

We hoped that placing the sickest behind screens would remove some of the fear among patients in the rest of the ward. We were badly wrong. Going through those red screens was seen as a death sentence. Blokes referred to them as the 'pearly gates' and 'gates to paradise' and quaked at the thought of being carried through them. A fellow might say: 'Oh God, another one's gone in; watch for him coming out feet first.' Men would plead not to go through the screens: 'No, no, I don't want to go, I'll never come out alive.' The experiment lasted for about a month before it was mercifully abandoned.

The intensity of working with dysentery patients was eased dramatically by an excellent doctor-nurse relationship. We formed sometimes bizarre teams working under difficult circumstances. In one ward at Roberts Hospital, doctors and orderlies shaved their heads both to prevent lice and as an expression of identity and pride in their collective endeavours. Doctors were generally distinguishable from orderlies only by their stethoscopes: almost every one – doctors and orderlies – wandered the wards in only shorts and worked to a small extent as fellow professionals, not as officers and men. This was a far cry from other areas of Changi where British military discipline was applied rigidly and officers swaggered around barking orders in their neatly ironed uniforms, seemingly oblivious to military failure and the end of empire.

Malaria

Malaria in its various forms, and in combination with dysentery and avitaminosis diseases, was the other scourge of the camps. There were many deaths. We now have an impression of Singapore as a modern, glittering financial, transport and services centre. In the 1940s it was far from that: anti-malaria measures in surrounding swampland had lapsed over a long period and malaria was endemic. If blokes didn't have mosquito nets and didn't take care, they got malaria. If they took care, like rolling down the flaps on their shorts at night to reduce exposure to bites or smearing on mosquito cream – which was truly horrible – or always sleeping under a net, some still got malaria.

Nursing patients with malaria required controlling shivering and violent shaking, but the basics again were not particularly complex. Blokes were given quinine, covered with blankets when they felt chilled and mopped down with cold water until their fevers broke. This would happen to each bloke at least once or twice a day, often more, and there were scores of blokes in a big ward needing attention both for malaria and anything else that ailed them. Doctors and orderlies were run off their feet.

I visited the malaria ward many times. On one occasion I visited a driver I knew who was dying from cerebral malaria. I sat down next to him when suddenly blood spurted from his nose and mouth. His spleen had burst. There was no doctor or ward orderly in the immediate area. Everyone was just too busy and, even if there had been, they couldn't have saved him.

Avitaminosis diseases

Many blokes, particularly those who experienced the very worst conditions of POW life in up-country sections of the railway in the summer of 1943, remember Changi as a golden period when they were not brutalised, had almost enough food and had access to medicine. That essentially is how I remember the hospital. If you had to be a prisoner, there were far worse places to be. Changi was not too bad and not too good. There was a lot of polished rice, albeit of very poor quality. The rice sometimes had a greenish tinge and smelt, possibly because it was treated with a chemical preservative. It was probably lime to control weevil infestation. The rice also was full of rat and mouse droppings and dead maggots. But after a while, we ate the lot and were grateful. We talked more and more about food, especially the lack of it, and less and less about football and women.

We were always hungry and, unlike in some other camps at Changi, couldn't get significant supplementation from outside working parties, though after a few weeks the Japanese did agree to parties going into Singapore to augment hospital rations. We also started growing vegetables, though not on the same scale as the Aussies, who quickly developed large gardens. I fantasised about eating something solid with a knife and fork: they are useless on rice and stew. I fantasised about bread and butter and cheese on toast. They became a symbol of luxury, steak an impossible dream.

Adjusting to a sharply reduced calorie intake and eating rice morning, noon and night was difficult for most men. My mother believed I would adapt easily to a rice diet because I liked rice pudding, but the logic doesn't hold. I sometimes vomited my evening meal during the early weeks of captivity, losing any goodness it contained. It was not long before insufficient vitamin B in the diet resulted in minor, though painful and persistent, ailments like mouth and throat ulcers, scrotal dermatitis and 'happy feet' – a very unpleasant burning sensation in the feet. I remember giving a jar of Marmite to one bloke with scrotal dermatitis and telling him to take a spoonful twice a day for a week and report back. He reported no improvement because he'd been smearing the precious stuff on his testicles! After a few months, serious deficiency diseases like beriberi and pellagra took hold. Around fifty to sixty blokes died of beriberi in the time I was at the hospital.

The problem of poor nourishment was not helped by the Japanese policy of giving half rations to sick men. The policy was based on the view that sickness resulted from weakness and lack of spirit and was an excuse for idleness. Malingers didn't need full rations and reduced rations provided an incentive for weak-spirited men to return to work and full rations. The policy was rubbish. Sick blokes just became sicker on a reduced version of the pathetic nourishment that was potentially available.

Oppression

There was a lot of death at Changi and much hard work, but there was no strong continuing sense of oppression like on the railway. Changi was so vast that, after a while, you didn't notice the wire around the perimeter or separating the hospital from the other camps unless you purposely looked for it or wanted to go to another area. Far more obvious was the physical beauty of this corner of Singapore Island. Weeks might go by without ever seeing Indian guards. Some Indian troops went over to the Japanese side to avoid captivity or because they were sick and tired of their colonial masters and saw the Japanese as liberators. I saw Indian guards only while being escorted or 'ferried' to the camp next door to see my friend Don Abbot. I recall seeing Japanese guards at the hospital once or twice between February and November 1942. I never saw Korean guards. The first time I saw them was at Ban Pong in southern Thailand.

Mental problems started to emerge slowly and there were a handful of suicides after about six months of captivity. One of our dysentery patients was among them. He jumped from a third-story balcony, narrowly missing a quartermaster sergeant taking a late night walk. The sergeant initially thought a mattress had fallen down while being aired, but soon discovered the young soldier. The British military police investigated but lost interest once they established he'd jumped and wasn't pushed.

As far as I'm aware there was no review of the general mental state of prisoners at this time, but several doctors warned us of a possible spike in suicides at the six-month mark. Several factors contributed to a growing sense of unease. The high incidence of disease, the inadequacy of food supplies, the large-scale redeployment of prisoners breaking up groups of friends, and separation from loved ones were perhaps the main ones. But the falseness of rumours of a Dunkirk-style rescue or of a winning British counter-offensive through Malaya – even the failure of sea battles like the Coral Sea and Midway in mid-1942 to secure our hoped for imminent release – all contributed to growing pessimism.

I was among a group of medics standing on top of our hospital building who saw elements of the Japanese fleet limping into Singapore harbour after the Battle of the Coral Sea. We were a long way away but saw badly damaged ships. Rumours inevitably started to swirl. The Japanese would pack it in. We would be free. Something good would happen next week or next month. But nothing happened. It was another let-down. About the only thing that can be ruled out as a contributor to the suicide spike is the unsettling effect of receiving disturbing letters from home. No mail was delivered during this period.

Rumours and the rest preyed on everyone's mind. Some of the pressures and disappointments seem silly in hindsight, but they weren't at the time. For a small minority, the let-downs extinguished hope and dashed expectations and became too hard to bear, but for the great bulk of blokes, or at least those I knew well, they were manageable. We reconciled ourselves to the facts that we were stuck, that it was going to be a long hard war – the war news filtering into the camp was not encouraging – and that release was years away. I thought about home and never doubted returning, but there wasn't much time for introspection. We were run off our feet with medical work. The routine kept us going: I think we were better off than blokes with time on their hands. Life for us was working, eating and sleeping. We didn't even have the concerts and education classes common in other parts of Changi. Monopoly was our principal distraction. We were smitten by it, sometimes staying up into the early hours of the morning to finish a game. There was a very strong desire to win and ostracism for anyone found cheating.

Our growing resilience or perhaps acceptance of the status quo helped us to cope with some nasty shocks in the second half of the year. At the start of September, four prisoners were executed on one of the beaches at Changi for attempting to escape. Some of our

45

officers witnessed the executions. They didn't provide details to the rank and file but said the executions were very messy. Rightly or wrongly we filled in the details, my group concluding that the blokes had been tied to stakes and used for target practice, starting with their feet and eventually being finished off with bayonets. The message went around that blokes shouldn't contemplate escape unless they were absolutely certain they could carry it off. The odds were stacked decisively against successful escapes: high levels of poverty among the local population increased the attractiveness of Japanese bounties paid on each escapee; many non-Chinese communities sympathised with the Japanese cause; it was more or less impossible to blend in with local populations; and friendly troops were hundreds of miles away across jungles and mountains in one direction and across an ocean in the other.

This was a dismal message but the impact on medical staff was arguably less than on other prisoners because we knew that our duty was to our patients and that we wouldn't attempt to escape. That had been drummed into us since the surrender. To some extent, therefore, we couldn't directly personalise the horror of what had befallen the four blokes because we knew we'd never run the risks they had.

The executions were followed immediately by the so-called Selarang Incident. For three days in early September, 16,000 men were crammed into the relatively small space of Selarang Barracks Square and weren't permitted to leave until they signed an undertaking not to escape. Latrines had to be dug next to the cookhouse – there was no other alternative – and a tidal wave of disease threatened. As it was there was a spike in dysentery and diphtheria, but it didn't persist. We medics didn't have to sign because the Japanese were informed we wouldn't attempt to escape. From the hospital at night I could see the lads' little lamps twinkling in the darkness and hear them singing. Ultimately, of course, the undertakings were all signed amid threats to cut rations and empty the hospital of its sick so they could join the throng on the barracks square. The undertakings therefore meant nothing because they were given under duress, and meant even less with so many Mickey Mouses and Donald Ducks in the ranks.

I still don't understand why the Japanese insisted on our blokes signing those worthless undertakings. Was it both to display and remind us of Japanese power and ruthlessness because we'd had so little contact with them over the preceding months? Was there a strategic dimension like attempting to free up Japanese forces from guarding prisoners who were regarded as the lowest of the low and worthless? Did their intentions become twisted into a stubborn face-saving exercise once our officers persistently refused to sign? It might have been all of these things, and perhaps others besides, but the incident was important. It could be seen simply as confirmation of our powerlessness and Japanese omnipotence, which it was. But, equally, it was a demonstration of our stiffening determination, courage and resolve. We weren't a tribe of strays any longer.

Leaving Changi

It came as no surprise in early November 1942 when I, along with over 8,000 others, was ordered to move out of Changi to an unknown destination. Groups had been leaving in large numbers for months and only about one-quarter to one-third of the original number of Changi POWs now remained.

I was glad to be leaving and so were my friends. We were stale and wanted a change, and it seemed that anything would be better than just endlessly repeating what we'd been doing there. Going to unknown places was adventurous: we were young and optimistic we'd survive and eventually be freed.

Chapter 4

From Bad to Worse

Standing at Singapore Railway Station on 5 November, my wife Marion's birthday, I was a mass of nervous tension. I might not have liked Changi and wanted to leave but it was a known quantity and wasn't all that bad apart from the appalling food, dysentery, diphtheria and beriberi. In one's flights of fancy, it was still conceivable that the British Army or the Royal Navy could mount a heroic rescue from Singapore, but it was inconceivable being rescued from the wilds of Asia.

I had no firm idea where we were going – rumour suggested southern Thailand – or what we would be doing. Again, rumour suggested work on the Burma-Thailand Railway, as had happened to those who'd gone before us. I also knew little about the Japanese. For many of us, this encounter at the railway station was our first with the Imperial Japanese Army since being marched away to captivity in mid-February. It was a salutary experience. Bewildered blokes milled around wondering what to do next. Japanese soldiers ran around with their little bamboo sticks, smacking anyone who didn't obey their incomprehensible orders immediately. Surly guards clarified orders with prods from rifle butts. There was much pushing, shoving and kicking. There were angry voices. And, somehow, order came from chaos and the train eventually set off. This was a nerve-racking beginning.

What eventually turned out to be a journey to Kanchanaburi – the principal base for the Burma-Thailand Railway project from early 1943 – took, in my case, about four months. The first stage was the train journey from Singapore to Ban Pong in southern Thailand. Ban Pong was the starting point of the new railway and the journey to it took place under foul, nightmarish conditions that count among my worst experiences as a POW. As luck would have it, the journey was followed by one of my very best experiences – four or five weeks of

48

recovery and good food at the small hospital camp at Ban Pong, fortunately some distance away from the otherwise squalid and dilapidated main transit camp. A short stay at the bug-infested hospital at Non Pladuk – a transport and logistics centre for the railway – completed my introduction to Thailand and preparations for the Kanchanaburi Hospital Camp.

Journey to Ban Pong

We were packed into closed railway wagons about 20 feet long by 10 feet wide. The floors, roofs and sides were all made from steel, as were the two sliding doors. In our party, around forty men were packed together in each wagon. This might have been a record of some kind: the average normally ranged from the mid-twenties to low thirties. Record or not, it was a damned uncomfortable jumble of legs and arms, bedrolls and backpacks. But what was galling at first was not the crush and the bad tempers it produced but a group of British officers, caricatures of the pre-war Army, who came to our wagon and ordered us to spread out through the train so they could disport themselves and their copious luggage – mattresses, camp beds, valises and kit – to their own satisfaction. They showed absolutely no regard for the fact that we were already packed in like sardines in a tin, would be even more tightly packed together after spreading through the train, and that even riff-raff needed an absolute minimum of space. They acted simply on the premise that they wanted to stay together as a group, and on a belief that they were entitled to more space and could do what they liked because, they too, for the most part, hadn't had much contact with the Imperial Japanese Army.

My one positive memory of that 5 November day is a Japanese private coming over to these officers and saying in passable English: 'I speak, forty men to one wagon.' He then ordered them back to their own wagon and to leave any excess luggage behind, apparently to be sent on later. This curtailment of British officer authority and privilege would have come as a shock. Times were changing.

The places favoured initially in the wagons were close to the walls so blokes had something solid to lean against and, notionally, could sleep better. These places were taken quickly and closely guarded. Unfortunately for the blokes grabbing them, the strategy backfired: the sides of the wagons became red hot during the day and ran with condensation at night, which soaked and chilled them. I sat near one of the sliding doors. This was not a popular choice at first. There were obvious disadvantages. There was a danger of falling out if the train jolted or lurched violently or if one fell asleep momentarily and slumped awkwardly. I put a string across the opening as an early warning device; it wouldn't have prevented a fall. There also was nothing to lean against except other blokes' backs. I leaned against big Luther Taylor, who nearly squashed me when he tried to sleep. Many arguments started this way, but the offsetting advantage of sitting by the doors was good ventilation. It was cool and fresh compared to the heat and reek inside the wagon. It also meant you could gaze out at the passing countryside – at the seemingly endless rubber plantations in Malaya and the jungle and paddy fields in Thailand – though by the time we reached Thailand my enthusiasm for the journey had evaporated and exhaustion bred indifference to the scenery and most other things.

Seating arrangements in the wagon inevitably created tension. The blokes on the sides wanted to move to places near the doors but we liked it where we were and wouldn't move. Conditions got worse as the five-day 900-mile journey wore on and blokes became more and more exhausted. Nobody really slept. You couldn't sleep. There was no place to lie down. Blokes raved at each other: 'Get out of my fucking way'; 'keep your bloody hands to yourself'; 'stop leaning on me, you bastard'. It became particularly bad when the guards locked the sliding doors as we passed through so-called sensitive areas or were shunted into sidings and temperatures soared inside the wagons.

Men with dysentery were in a dreadful state: they weren't generally seriously ill but it was very inconvenient and embarrassing for them. My friend Nightingale (Nighty) came down with it. He had to be held firmly by both arms with someone holding him round the waist as he squatted in a moving train over the edge of the sliding metal doors. He was such an exceptionally clean man and was so embarrassed by it all. Many others performed the same gymnastic feats or combined them with other strategies. Nighty found a kind of woven bamboo bowler hat that served as a toilet for part of the journey. When it was full he threw it out of the wagon, chuckling in anticipation that someone might pick it up, thinking it was their lucky day, only to have a rude shock.

The train stopped from time to time for water and coal at designated halts, including the big stations going up Malaya – Gemas,

Kuala Lumpur, Ipoh, Prai. The English names were still proudly visible and some of the stations looked like those back in Britain, presumably because they had been designed by British architects and built by British engineers and construction companies. This struck me forcefully at Ipoh. We arrived at night and the station lights were on. For a moment or two I felt I was back in England. We stopped two or three times in Thailand but I don't remember the station names. There were no signs in English.

All the stops had a similar sense of urgency about them. Blokes ran to the toilet or to whatever might serve their need. Two or three whistles from the train brought everyone back again. We moved quickly, even with trousers flapping around our ankles. Mates pulled friends on board if the train was moving. No one wanted to be left behind and risk being charged with attempted escape.

The potential for food and water stops to become scrums was largely avoided. To a small extent this was because the Japanese distributed Red Cross food parcels at the start of the journey. About eight blokes shared a parcel meant for one, so there wasn't an abundance of food – just a few spoonfuls per person from each tin – but it was something.

Distributing food parcels on this journey may have been standard Japanese policy judging by the number of tin cans littering the track. To a much greater extent, the relative calm at feeding time was the outcome of reasonable planning. Bamboo skips of fried rice and containers of water were set out at designated railway stations. Two men from each wagon were responsible for bringing a bucketful of rice and one of water to the wagon. The Japanese ordered a maximum of five men (representing five different wagons) to fill their rice buckets from a given skip at any one time. This was clear, though the officers were slow off the mark at the first food stop, perhaps waiting for batmen who never arrived. A lieutenant eventually appeared, bucket in hand. He went frantically from skip to skip only to be told: 'Fuck off mate, it's five to a skip.' He probably didn't get much food for his fellow officers. The bluntness of the men's response to this officer was remarkable. It wouldn't have happened at Changi.

While the journey to Ban Pong was grim with blokes going down with mild dysentery and malaria by the score and everyone suffering from the effects of prolonged sleep deprivation, it had a lighter side, like when Ben Adam, our pharmacist, strolled towards the guards van at Ipoh and an absent-minded guard handed him his rifle. But by far the best part of the journey – excluding when at last it finished and before the Japanese ordered us to march to camp – was trading for fruit.

There was little or no trading on the Malayan leg of the journey. Perhaps the Malays had no love for their former colonial masters and were happy to see the back of us. The Thais, on the other hand, showed no reticence. At sidings or stations, traders and farmers crept up to the wagons on whatever side the guards were not looking, released the bolts and opened the sliding doors. Language was no barrier. Buyer and seller quickly got the idea. One shirt bought one very large basket of fruit, which was then shared among friends. We discovered later that a shirt was worth three baskets, but to me that revelation didn't undo the pleasure of those initial exchanges. They were most welcome and unexpected episodes in an otherwise gruelling and soulless journey.

Ban Pong

On 10 November we arrived at Ban Pong completely exhausted. Medics were assigned to the small 'hospital' camp – just two huts and a cookhouse – on the outskirts of the town on the road to Non Pladuk. We were ordered to march there. It seemed a long way away because we were exhausted and carrying our kit, though in reality it was only a mile or two. Once at the camp we slept around the clock.

In the cold light of morning, the hospital camp wasn't inspiring. The two huts were typical of POW huts everywhere in the region. They were long and narrow and had attap roofs; bed platforms were at knee height and ran lengthwise along both sides of the hut; each man had about 2 feet by 6 feet of sleeping and living space; and there was a narrow passageway in the middle separating the two lines of bed platforms. The hospital had about 100 mostly 'light sick' patients – blokes who had come up from Singapore on various working parties, developed dysentery or malaria on the way and needed a few recovery days before rejoining their units, usually at Non Pladuk or Kanchanaburi. Through Japanese intransigence there was a pitiful supply of medicines, lotions and basics like bandages and gauze, so it was fortunate that the great bulk of our patients weren't too sick.

The hospital was infested with bugs, though not on a scale that caused too much distress, and wasn't improved when it was briefly flooded two weeks into our stay. Clean water wasn't available locally, so it meant a lot of extra walking and carrying; for a time warm food wasn't available because the cookhouse fires were all out; disposing of dysentery discharges involved trekking to higher ground; and looking after patients marooned on their raised sleeping platforms required sloshing around in filthy water up to our knees. But for all its shortcomings, the hospital camp had three overwhelming merits.

First, it was not anywhere near as bad as the large Ban Pong transit camp half a mile away. That camp was on slightly lower ground, was partly under water even before the flood and was a breeding ground for malaria. Some huts had collapsed and those still standing were mostly decrepit. The place was squalid and insanitary. It was a glorified midden.

Second, we were not overrun with patients either from the train or the main transit camp. Dysentery was the principal worry but no one died in the few weeks I was at Ban Pong because blokes were reasonably fit when they left Singapore. In my view the dysentery situation at Ban Pong was better than at Changi. Malaria was a problem. There weren't enough drugs, half the blokes didn't have mosquito nets and the sodden farmland was an ideal breeding ground for mosquitoes. Fortunately, we didn't have to cope with the worst malarias. We faced challenges with skin diseases like scabies, eczema and tinea because of our limited medical supplies. But all in all, the medical situation wasn't bad. Blokes were recovering all the time and were being sent on their way. Only a handful of more serious cases remained and accompanied us to Non Pladuk at the end of the year.

Third, unlike the transit camp, the hospital camp wasn't sealed in by rolls of barbed wire and there were no guards. Guards walked around the camp perimeter once a day, looked in but never entered, and then walked to the market square in the village to stop any blatant selling of shirts and shorts. There was no evening roll-call. We didn't bother the guards and they didn't bother us as long as we were polite and bowed to them. We were unfettered, almost free. We didn't feel like prisoners.

This comparative freedom produced big dividends. I palled up with Robbie (Robinson), a bloke from Bedford I'd known vaguely in the 198th Field Ambulance in England but who was to become as close to me as a brother over the next year. We were free to roam in our spare time and experience some of the sights, sounds and smells of southern Thailand – a delight in itself and wonderful after the confinement and routine of Changi.

Like everyone else, Robbie and I exchanged clothes at Ban Pong for large amounts of fruit and other foods, which we shared. Food was abundant and very welcome after the strictures of Changi: rice paddies stretched out in every direction; livestock was raised intensively; products like meat, milk and eggs were plentiful; and there was a super abundance of good vegetables and fruit. Thai women from a nearby *kampong* often came to the perimeter of the hospital camp with fruit and delicious dishes of curried chicken and fish: the spices were wonderful. We also went to the market – a cluster of stalls dotted around a school or community centre – to buy fruit and particularly to sample the local cuisine. There were waffles, fried bananas, sweet peanut dishes and my favourite, something called '*marme*'. It was like tagliatelle made from tapioca with spring onions, cunning spices and two eggs. It was vastly better than the rubbish we'd been eating at Changi or the meals prepared in the hospital camp cookhouse. The interlude at Ban Pong was almost the only time in my POW years when I didn't have to depend on the cookhouse and never watched each serving of rice and stew like a hawk.

Bartering for food was the best approach for all concerned. The Thais were reluctant to accept the Japanese-backed currency in which our 'wages' were paid because they instinctively realised the Japanese could print as much money as they liked and it wasn't a real store of value. From our point of view, there were risks in holding Thai currency because we could only have acquired it by selling our clothes. As far as the Japanese were concerned, this was theft of their property and warranted a bashing for the guilty.

While food was always uppermost in our thoughts, the freedom given to us at Ban Pong allowed us to go on walks through the countryside, look at local temples and, most spectacularly, experience the colour, noise and vibrancy of Thai culture. Nowadays, most people in the West have some knowledge of Thai culture through television, the Internet and often through tourism and business. In the 1940s, awareness was limited to a few travellers, bureaucrats and academics, and very little was known about Thailand in the broader community. I was fascinated by Thai funerals with trumpeters leading the procession to drive away evil spirits; professional mourners in sacking, weeping and wailing; the open coffin done out with wallpaper; strings from the deceased's fingers reaching out to the descendants' (presumably symbolising physical and spiritual linkages); relatives laughing and talking; saffron-robed priests chanting and receiving food offerings from the family; coconut milk poured over the head of the deceased (perhaps as a final farewell drink); the coffin placed on top of a funeral pyre built straight up, with stakes in the ground to hold it in place; and, finally, family members lighting the pyre with sprigs of bamboo made into flowers.

Like many others, I regarded the month or so at the Ban Pong Hospital Camp as a period of physical and psychological recovery, of fattening up and rebuilding of strength to face an uncertain future. It was by far the best time I spent as a prisoner.

Non Pladuk

In the week before Christmas 1942 my unit left the Ban Pong Hospital Camp with a handful of seriously ill patients and went by truck the short distance to Non Pladuk. This was by far my worst camp in forty-two months as a prisoner.

Construction of the Non Pladuk working camp started in mid-1942. By the time I arrived, it was a sizeable camp with base workshops and stores for the railway project. It was a hive of activity, mostly involving heavy work. Trains were arriving loaded with supplies of everything from drums of oil and track-laying equipment to nails and food. Unloading was done in quick time and trains sped off for more supplies. Blokes were loading sleepers and rails onto trains that carried them to construction sites up the line. Parts were being manufactured, others fixed and then transported to yet more construction sites as part of the gigantic Japanese plan to connect Singapore, Bangkok and Burma; bolster their position in Burma as reinforcement by sea became increasingly difficult after Midway; and develop a launching pad to attack India.

Non Pladuk was a working camp for fit blokes. There was nothing elaborate about the camp hospital, at least in my time there. It was no more than a sick bay accommodating up to 100 patients at one end of a large hut. There were a few desperately ill patients, and medical supplies were limited. There was quinine for malaria but nothing like emetine for treating dysentery, which once again was the principal problem. The hospital, however, sticks in my memory for two reasons. I spent my first Christmas there as a prisoner, an event marked by a Canadian officer leading lusty singing of *God Save the King*, Korean guards rushing in at the double with fixed bayonets, strident orders to stop singing, and bashings for the laggards. *Land of Hope and Glory* and *There'll Always be an England* were deemed to be acceptable alternatives and were sung instead.

The main reason I remember the hospital is the unimaginable scale of bug infestation. Bugs and lice, of course, were a standard part of POW life. You expected bugs in the bedding and would pop them. You expected lice, and blokes might 'groom' each other as they lined up for food. But the infestation in this hospital was off any conceivable scale. Robbie and I went on night duty as soon as we arrived at the hospital. Robbie sat on a stool and started reading a book. After a few minutes bugs were literally crawling up his legs and scampering on the book. He went mad. He clawed at his shorts. When that didn't work, he dropped them and started hammering at his legs and thighs. By this time I also was dancing and stamping my feet to keep the bugs away. It was exhausting having to maintain this through the night.

The other medics who'd been with us at Ban Pong didn't fare much better. They bunked down in one corner of the hospital hut and set up a large green mosquito net supplied by the Japanese. After a few minutes they too started leaping about and alarmed voices were saying things like: 'Bugger me, bugger me, what the fuck's happening?' The patients weren't having a good time either. I don't know anything about the previous medical staff at Non Pladuk but they couldn't have been up to much: patients were cursing loudly and in some cases leaping and writhing in response to the ordeal of the bugs. The worse case was a patient who was both paralysed and suffering from one of the avitaminosis diseases. He was lying on a stretcher and must have been sleeping under the same blanket for weeks. It was infested with lice and bugs and, being paralysed, he hadn't noticed the bites or, if had, hadn't complained loud enough. In the morning we took his blanket outside and it shimmered with lice in the sunlight.

That first night of battling bugs was enough torment. For the medics, it was simple enough to sleep outside for a while in a shelter we built quickly with a bamboo frame, split banana tree trunks for walls, thatched banana leaves for the roof, and our groundsheets for a floor. Far more difficult was to deal with infestation in the hospital. A proposal was put to the Japanese to take up the floorboards. They agreed and a working party was reassigned for one day from the railway martialling yards to work at the hospital. The floorboards were removed and thick masses of reddish black bugs and white eggs were exposed where the boards went over the joists. Smoky fires were built outside the huts and the thick boards were passed through them. Nothing could be done with the walls and the attap. Treating them would have required demolishing the huts, which the Japanese wouldn't have permitted.

Some improvement was achieved. The level of infestation was reduced. There was less endless scratching and fewer mysterious recurrent fevers, and we put a temporary end at least to bugs crawling up blokes' legs. We medics bunked down in the hospital again but the morning rituals of spreading out mosquito nets and clothing and letting strong sunlight shrivel up abundant bugs, eggs and lice remained strictly in force.

The Non Pladuk hospital was an awful place at this time – and perhaps later – because of the desperate struggle against insect infestation. My New Year's wish in 1943 was to get out of Non Pladuk as fast as I could. I hated the camp and resented the fact that I'd drawn the short straw to remain there while the rest of my unit moved to Kanchanaburi. My wish to leave came true about two months later. I was jubilant and relieved when at last I received orders to proceed to the Kanchanaburi Hospital Camp. Good or bad, it had to be an improvement.

Chapter 5

Avalanche of Disease

By the time the truck carrying me from Non Pladuk lumbered into Kanchanaburi in mid-March 1943, the town was being transformed from a small sleepy provincial capital into a centre of activity supporting the railway project. The population of the town and its immediate hinterland had doubled or trebled in the previous few months. Working parties of prisoners laboured laying tracks, extending work camps and transporting supplies for major undertakings like completing the steel bridge over the Khwae Mae Khlong at Tamarkan – the infamous bridge over the River Kwai.

In line with accelerating activity on the railway, the Kanchanaburi Hospital Camp grew and changed quickly. Lieutenant Colonel Malcolm, RAMC, started the hospital camp in late 1942. By Christmas, it consisted of two large wards, each about 100 yards long, with two rows of sleeping platforms in the centre (with blokes sleeping head to head in herringbone fashion), two rows down each side, two aisles separating the central and side sleeping platforms, and an orderly station about halfway down the ward, where medicines and equipment were stored.

By the time I arrived, there were four sizeable wards and a central complex, part providing accommodation for officers, part used as an administrative centre and the remainder housing the operating theatre, the pharmacy, a laboratory for analysing blood and faecal samples, and a dental surgery. A month or so later, two more large wards were added. By this time the hospital had become one of the 'cities of the sick', one of the key base hospitals in southern Thailand and, arguably, its principal medical centre. Patients were predominantly British, with some Aussies and a few dozen older Dutch Javanese who should never have been brought out to work on the railway.

Peak disease

Nineteen-forty-three stands out for me as the peak year for disease. At the start of the year, there were several hundred patients in the hospital camp. Diseases like dysentery, malaria, diphtheria, beri-beri, and pellagra were almost out of control. Virtually everyone succumbed to malaria in one form or another, though thankfully strains like cerebral malaria and blackwater fever were rare. Every-one came down with dysentery. All it took was a lapse in hygiene and just bad luck, as in the case of my friend, Corporal Norman Aldridge, from Otley, in Yorkshire. He was a medical orderly in the dysentery ward. One morning he invited me for 'coffee' – a con-coction of burnt rice and water sweetened with molasses. He used one of two mugs that had been crawling with flies. I told him I wouldn't have anything from those mugs. He laughed, saying I shouldn't be afraid and needed to toughen up to the conditions. A few days later he had terrible dysentery and within a fortnight was dead.

Diphtheria was an ongoing problem. Blokes came down with it in the surrounding work camps and were treated at the hospital with mixed results. Many died. Avitaminosis diseases were rampant and similarly accounted for many deaths. In addition, there were a host of lesser diseases. Everybody had dengue fever at one time or another and things like worm infestation were commonplace. We were spared respiratory diseases like tuberculosis, despite the over-crowding, because our huts were open-sided and therefore natu-rally ventilated. I recall only one case of tuberculosis at the hospital camp – a young officer who was isolated for months at one end of the dysentery ward.

By mid-year, the hospital camp had over 1,000 patients and this number rose during the monsoon months – basically May to September, with July and August the rainiest months – as patients arrived by train and barge from up-country work camps with a variety of diseases and, in many cases, tropical ulcers on their legs and feet. Under prevailing conditions in those work camps, cuts or bites often turned into ulcers, which could grow from a speck to as big as a saucer in a few weeks. The men arrived in a dreadful state, a picture of utter misery and desperation on a scale I'd not seen before. In one memorable trainload carrying about 100 wretches, a few were dead; some had ulcers stretching from ankle to knee revealing the structure of bones and joints and could have been living exhibits on human anatomy; some had bones sticking out of feet in place of toes; one or two had ulcerated eyes. Almost all were silent with heads on upraised knees clutching diseased legs or feet, their whole bodies rigid from lack of movement. They were soaked in excrement, covered in lice and stank of gangrene. They must have been in that state for weeks. How they'd slept and functioned I don't know. And they were the tip of an iceberg. The mortality rate among them was very high.

Cholera followed hard on the heels of the ulcer cases. Everyone dreaded its arrival. During May, June and July we heard sketchy reports of the disease's progress through the river catchment systems in the upper and middle sections of the railway, and of diseased, overworked men being pushed beyond their endurance in conditions of great filth, starvation and contaminated water supplies. Even more frightening for us were stories, often relayed by British and Aussie drivers for the Japanese, of cholera outbreaks and deaths lower down the catchment at nearby camps like Tarsau and Chungkai. These stories became more compelling and urgent when one of our medics contracted cholera and died while on temporary secondment to a hospital up the line. Our hospital camp had an isolated outbreak, mercifully on a far smaller scale than at other base hospitals and especially the up-country work camps.

More patients arrived from up-country camps during the last quarter of 1943, after the completion of the railway, but not in the same numbers as earlier arrivals. Base hospitals higher up the line probably took the bulk of them and some of the worst cases might have been too sick to travel and died at hospitals up-country. This was a relief for us. By the end of the year, the hospital camp's cemetery was populated well enough.

Causes of the avalanche
All manner of diseases exploded in Southeast Asia in 1943. My rationalisation of the small part I saw is as follows. Health and well-being were declining through 1942. This fact was clear at Roberts Hospital from the deadly toll taken by dysentery, malaria, diphtheria, and beriberi. It also was clear from more subtle evidence of ill health among POWs as indicated by significant weight loss, multiple episodes of mild malaria and dysentery, and the rapid spread of skin diseases of one sort or another. Things like weight loss and mild malaria were not directly life threatening. Blokes put

up with them and got on with their lives, but they were debilitating, reduced well-being and chipped away at resilience to withstand major episodes of disease later on.

Health and well-being continued to decline through 1943, the cumulative result of slow starvation, lack of medicines and Japanese indifference to POW welfare. Work on the railway intensified as the Japanese pushed single-mindedly to complete it as quickly as possible. This, coupled with declining resilience and the extra physical demands of overwork under wet season conditions, set the stage for general ill health and mortality rates to soar. Rapid growth in patient numbers at the Kanchanaburi Hospital Camp was one indicator, among many, of this upsurge. But this indicator can't explain the real tragedy that overwhelmed men in up-country work camps. Conditions in southern Thailand were bad but nowhere near as bad as those up-country.

As work pressures eased later in the year, the pace of deterioration in general health levels slowed and then stabilised. The intensity and scale of suffering would never be as bad again, though conditions comparable to the 'speedo' period* of railway construction in the middle months of 1943 did exist from time to time in different areas and produced localised spikes in ill health and death rates. My worst time as a POW was in central Thailand in the last six or seven months of the war and I was fortunate to survive. But in general, if you survived 1943 in reasonable shape, you survived the war.

Lack of food

Long term starvation was the main cause of disease and death among a weakening population of prisoners. I never saw a 'fat' man die. The ones who died usually were the thinnest. Some were like the pictures of Belsen victims that so horrified the post-war world. The food situation at the hospital camp was atrocious. Following standard policy, the Japanese authorities put the sick on half rations, guaranteeing unnecessary deaths or difficult and slow recoveries for those who survived. The medical staff received full rations but we all ate from the same pot, so we too were effectively on half rations.

*The speedo period was when the Japanese leadership advanced the completion date for the railway from December to August 1943: the railway was eventually completed in mid-October.

From the perspective of the hospital camp, the food at Changi didn't seem so bad after all: there'd been a bit more meat there and there was slightly more variation in the otherwise endless regime of rice and green vegetable soup.

A typical day revolved around food. Breakfast was thin rice gruel, sometimes with salt added – we always kept rock salt handy for those occasions when it wasn't available – and a small helping of stew. On a good morning, a bit of sugar would be added. This was washed down with a pint of weak tea – effectively, flavoured boiled water – without sugar or milk, or sometimes 'coffee' made from burnt rice. We would work on the wards until lunchtime. Lunch was a mug of tea and a more solid helping of white rice and a small amount of green stew with a smattering of sweet potato, radish or aubergine, and might include an egg from time to time. We'd then go back to the wards. The evening meal was similar, except that shreds of meat or fish might flavour the stew. Day shift medics often then returned to the wards. At the end of the day everyone remained hungry.

In almost a year at the hospital camp, this routine never changed, though the supply of meat or fish increased at odd times. On one or two occasions, boxes of small fish, prawns and dried fish were provided by the Japanese. The Dutch Javanese collected the fish bones, fried them until brown and crisp and then ate them, probably for the calcium. I don't recall any other instance when the Japanese supplied additional food to the entire camp, though they did provide eggs occasionally for the 'heavy sick'. Nor do I recall the distribution of Red Cross parcels at this time. They typically contained chocolate, oatmeal, biscuits, tins of sardines, and dried fruit, as well as medical supplies, clothing and footwear, cigarettes, toiletries, and reading material. The food presumably was eaten by the guards or sold to traders, and the other items might have been sold or stored. I never heard of Japanese or Korean guards stealing any of our standard food rations, though they may have. They ate better quality rice than we did, so if rice or other food were stolen, it would have been sold.

On other occasions when additional food was supplied to the entire camp, the source was the Red Cross. They supplied a half-starved, but well appreciated, bullock. Our butchers tied its feet together, threw it on its side, slit the jugular vein, and collected the blood in a large bowl. Nothing was wasted. The butchering process was horrible to watch, even for blokes accustomed to seeing death, but the bullock helped to produce a decent stew for 1,000 or so hungry men. The Red Cross also supplied three or four pigs, which were fed on vegetable peelings for a time, killed and put in the pot. Again, they produced an acceptable stew.

Blokes were always looking to supplement their rations. Buying eggs was a priority. Eggs were plentiful in southern Thailand. The problem was whether you or your mates had the money to buy them either from the camp's canteen at inflated prices or from blokes on working parties who traded at local *kampongs*. Without money you remained hungry. With money, you could share a fried egg and rice biscuit and be less hungry.

It took ingenuity to ward off starvation. One opportunity was provided by the Japanese issuing some of us with Javanese clothing – green trousers, jackets and hats. It happened only once and the clothes were sold quickly to Thais in Kanchanaburi. We received good money and spent it on food. Another more dangerous opportunity was when some blokes started stealing Javanese clothing being stockpiled by the Japanese under large tarpaulins near the hospital camp's guardroom – an area used for morning and evening roll-calls. The clothing stockpile diminished rapidly, the tarpaulins started to sag and half the residents of Kanchanaburi seemed to be dressed in Javanese clothes. The Japanese inevitably checked the stockpile, revealed the extent of the theft and ordered everyone out on parade. We went with hats, shirts and water bottles expecting to be there all day and perhaps all night or longer until someone, or some group, owned up. It had to be an inside job: it defied credibility that Thais would have sneaked into a guarded camp to pilfer bulky goods from in front of the guardroom. As it turned out, we stood at attention for the best part of twenty-four hours, no one owned up and the Japanese never resolved the 'crime'. Relations with the Japanese deteriorated and any small leeway to augment camp food rations disappeared for a while.

Lack of medicines and other medical supplies

Ben Adam, our Scottish pharmacist, brought up medical supplies to the hospital camp from Changi early in 1943. They came in stout boxes and probably filled a standard railway truck, but there was never a period at the hospital camp when medicines were in reasonable supply. From the outset, they were eked out very carefully for they were precious: demand always exceeded supply; there was an expectation that demand would increase as general standards of health and well-being declined; there was little prospect of procuring further supplies from Singapore; and the Japanese provided limited assistance relative to their capability and couldn't be relied on to release medical supplies from Red Cross parcels. Medical goods, for the most part, were barely adequate and sometimes nearly ran out. Doctors had to work creatively, and often at personal risk, to augment supplies.

On the positive side, the Japanese supplied large quantities of quinine, which was understandable because they had conquered territory that produced the bulk of the world's supply. The problem was that men were constantly coming down with malaria, which strained the relationship between supply and demand. The Japanese supplied dressings, a seemingly endless quantity of creosote pills (which tasted as good as they sounded and weren't especially effective in treating diarrhoea and dysentery), a Lysol type of disinfectant, and cholera and dysentery vaccines because they didn't want slave diseases killing them. The hospital also had reasonable supplies of bandages and gauze, magnesium sulphate for treating dysentery, potassium permanganate and formalin for treating tinea, chlordane and kaolin for treating stomach problems, and mild antiseptic such as Mercurochrome, sulphur mixtures and salicylic acid.

Most other things were in short supply or not available. Supplies of emetine, used for treating amoebic and other forms dysentery, were always limited. I was rarely told by doctors to give emetine to patients and those who did receive it probably never had a full course. I was never privy as to how emetine came into the hospital but understand it involved bartering quinine for emetine with the Thais. M&B 693 – also used in treating dysentery – was a rarity at Kanchanaburi. I'm not aware of specialist drugs being available for treating diphtheria. There was a chronic shortage of dressings like iodoform for treating ulcer patients, though the situation was better for sulphanilamide. There were no supplies of general anaesthetic. Operations to remove feet and legs took place using local anaesthetics in the lower back. Supplies of anaesthetics like Novocain were limited. The dental surgeon even ran out of cocaine to deaden the pain of teeth extraction and repair. Patients just had to put up with the pain, though a visiting Japanese senior officer, who suffered the ordeal, facilitated additional supplies that lasted for a month or two.

In an environment of great suffering, where much of the medical cupboard lay bare, basic psychology came to play an ever greater role in motivating less seriously ill patients and nudging them in the direction of recovery.

Indifference to suffering

To Japanese leaders, and those down the chain of command, POWs were an inexhaustible supply of free labour and our lives and health were inconsequential. We were expendable. I never saw the full measure of this indifference to starvation and overwork. To do so, I'd have to have laboured on the railway during the worst months of 1943. Almost one half of POWs labouring on the middle and upper sections of the railway in northern Thailand died during the speedo period. This death rate compares to perhaps ten per cent or less in the base areas.

What I saw in the Kanchanaburi Hospital Camp and in work camps later on was Japan's total contempt for sickness. As indicated previously, sickness was equated with dishonour and shame and even with sabotage if it created problems in filling the day's work quota. In their distorted view, the justification for sending sick and starving men to work in sometimes appalling conditions may have been to make unworthy men more worthy. The facts that it killed many of them and that human beings work better if they are reasonably well fed, have access to medicine and are not grossly overworked, never challenged this dogma.

The mixture of indifference and contempt often was a precursor to violence. The hospital camp had its fair share of broken arms, legs and noses, but it wasn't a work camp and the level of violence was nowhere near the scale reported in up-country camps. I didn't come across many Japanese guards at the hospital camp. There were a few privates, the *gunso* and, from afar, the camp commandant. The guards were mainly Koreans and their behaviour was mixed. There were a few decent individuals. Some seemed to be victims of Japanese ill-treatment and simply passed it on to those of lower status than themselves. Most were easily provoked and resorted to violence in the blinking of an eye. I haven't a good word to say for them. Not bowing to them or not bowing quickly enough or precisely enough could set them off in a tirade of violence.

The 'Undertaker' was a vicious and unpleasant bastard and the worst guard I encountered in my POW years. He was a tall Korean who relished his nickname: he claimed 'All men call me Undertaker'. This was at least partly correct. We heard other Korean guards using the nickname but the few Japanese at the camp were so disdainful of Koreans in general they probably hardly ever spoke to him. Regardless, the nickname was well deserved. The Undertaker boasted of killing two prisoners for disobedience. We knew he'd helped to beat a British sergeant major to a pulp who'd been implicated in using a secret radio. The Undertaker was a man you tried to avoid at all costs.

I was badly beaten only once. I was collecting water from a well just outside the camp boundary and didn't bow to a Korean guard because he was some distance away. There was a long queue and I joined the end of it. The guard called me over. He was standing under a canopy fitted over the well, which was just a hole in the ground without a protective wall. He asked me if I understood why he'd called me. I said I didn't. With his left fist he hit me on the jaw as hard as he could, nearly knocking me down the well. The fellows at the well stopped me from falling in. He then asked if I understood. I said I did so he hit me hard with his right fist for understanding. He then started bashing me with his rifle butt. You couldn't defend yourself because this would be interpreted as an attack and would result in a bigger beating inside the guardroom. The lads, thank God, picked me up and got me out of the way because there was no telling how far the guard might have gone: by this stage he was out of control. I ran off with an empty bucket. After that the guard came looking for me every day. I avoided him with help from blokes who acted as lookouts.

Looking back on it, bowing properly to the guards was nothing more than showing basic courtesy, like saluting an officer or tipping one's hat to a lady. That was how the guards saw it. But that wasn't how we saw it. Part of our problem was our chauvinistic attitude. We were British or Aussies or whatever, and didn't bow to anyone. Part reflected lingering rancour over Singapore: a British general had surrendered but somehow we, the rank and file, hadn't. Bowing smacked of personal submission and it rankled. One serious beating was enough to convince most sensible people that this wasn't smart thinking. A bad beating could be a death sentence.

POWs and Asian labourers

Lack of decent food, lack of medicine, overwork, and growing brutality can be distilled to a central proposition: in pursuit of their political and military objectives, the Japanese leadership was indifferent to the plight and suffering of POWs and the 200,000–300,000 Asian labourers who worked on the railway. Twenty per cent of prisoners and around fifty per cent of Asian labourers died on the railway compared with about seven per cent of guards.

In 1944 I saw several Japanese camps while on working parties in the Kanchanaburi region. The Japanese were typically fit and healthy and well fed. They ate good rice, fish, prawns, and beautifully cooked vegetables. And they were so clean, often walking around after bathing with white fluffy towels around their necks.

The contrast in living conditions between these Japanese camps and POW camps was stark but we at least had doctors, medical facilities and an organisational structure that helped us to cope with the challenges produced by Japan's fixation on completing the railway at any cost in the shortest possible time. Having those structures in place greatly reduced the overall level of ill health and mortality rates among POWs.

The contrast between living conditions in the Japanese camps and the plight of Asian labourers was almost unimaginable. The labourers were a collection of individuals, families and disparate groups that had been brought together to work on the railway. They were not organised and had no means of becoming organised. They were cast adrift without any support networks. I came across one party of Asian labourers in an isolated part of Kanchanaburi. There were several dozen Tamils, Malays and others crammed into a large hut. They were all desperately ill. The first thing I thought of was cholera, but they could have been suffering from anything. I didn't dare go too near them. They had no food or water. They'd served their purpose. They were expendable.

67

Chapter 6

Kanchanaburi Hospital Camp

The hospital camp was no shining beacon of tropical medicine. Like the other base hospitals in southern Thailand, it didn't have reserves of specialist doctors (eye specialists, surgeons, neurologists, specialists in tropical medicine), general practitioners or highly trained medical orderlies from the Regular Army. It lacked modern medical equipment and technology – a microscope for analysing blood and stool samples was about as far as our technology went – and there was no electricity. Food was always limited and essential medical supplies were either non-existent or far from assured. By any standards, the hospital camp was primitive. It certainly seemed so in comparison with Roberts Hospital, whose rapid rise was based on gathering and harnessing the technology and professional and administrative expertise from Singapore's military hospitals.

What the hospital camp did have, in common with other base hospitals, was a solid core of dedicated doctors and medics who were committed to saving lives, and the organisation to perform a range of functions that were difficult or impossible to perform in the medical units of jungle camps. The camp made a difference to people's lives. Potentially the greatest impact came through successful operations that relieved pain and gave patients a new chance at life. Mostly the medical staff worked hard just to hold the line against diseases like malaria and dysentery, recognising that full recoveries were rare and relapses inevitable given lack of resources. Escalating patient numbers sometimes overwhelmed stretched resources, undermined any pretence of good patient care and resulted in needless deaths. Making a difference then came down to showing care and compassion in the final stages of life, though even this was difficult at times. On occasions there were just too many critically sick men and men died alone.

The medical team

The hospital camp had a small complement of doctors in relation to the number of patients and its importance for the railway. The doctors were impressive. Lieutenant Colonel Malcolm (RAMC) was the camp's chief medical officer. He was a surgeon but spent most of his time running the hospital and securing additional supplies of food and medicine. Seen from afar, he seemed to be in constant meetings with the Japanese commandant, presumably seeking concessions of one sort or another. The hospital ran well under his leadership. Major de Soldinoff (RAMC) was an excellent doctor and surgeon and a fine man. He wandered around the wards with such authority, strength, confidence, and purpose. His inspiration kept blokes going. It was a privilege to know him. Lieutenant C.J. Poh (SSVF) worked mainly on dysentery and malaria. He combined quiet professionalism and sympathy in his lengthy chats with patients. At times sympathy was all he, or any one else, could offer. Two Anglo-Indian doctors (I only remember 'Dr Mac') specialised in tropical medicine and worked principally on the dysentery ward. They were highly skilled, engaging and established a strong rapport with patients. A microbiologist dealt with blood and dysentery samples. And the highly likeable dental surgeon, Jimmy, handled all the dentistry. I had the greatest respect for them all.

About forty medics supported these doctors. A few were highly skilled such as Jock Lynas, Blackpool Football Club's pre-war trainer, who was the masseuse and had been a radiographer at Roberts Hospital; Ben Adam, our pharmacist; Bill Graham, the head orderly on the surgical ward; and the dental mechanic. The other medics had the same basic training as me and many had only reached third class nursing orderly.

As patient numbers climbed in mid-1943 and the number of medical staff remained stationary, twenty to forty men from the infantry, Engineers and other units volunteered for medical work at various times. They were courageous men who were prepared to put themselves at risk. Some had knowledge of first aid, having served as regimental stretcher bearers. They made a substantial contribution, particularly by doing some awful jobs like emptying bed pans (when we had them), helping patients to the latrines in the middle of the night and preparing men for burial.

Pulling together

The medical team worked long hours. Doctors took responsibility for a ward or a section of a ward and were on call twenty-four hours a day. In practice, night work was limited to responding to unexpected and dangerous gyrations in patients' health: most deaths were predictable and doctors were not routinely required to confirm death. Medics worked twelve-hour shifts with day and night shifts merging as circumstances required: there was no strict time keeping. Weekend work was the norm. Life revolved around the hospital. There were no concerts and few visits to Kanchanaburi, even though the town was only a mile away from the hospital. Free time was spent sleeping, playing fiercely competitive games of bridge and discussing the latest news and rumours, which circulated as fast as in any other camp.

The medical team had a strong sense of cohesion based around respect for life and doing the best that was possible to alleviate suffering. The military hierarchy among the doctors didn't get in the way of their good-natured co-operative approach to medicine, though it did marginalise the Anglo-Indian doctors. Amazingly, these excellent physicians were warrant officers, not commissioned officers. It was a terrible slight and they must have bridled at the injustice. They were treated with respect by their peers on the wards but were then not permitted to eat with them or sleep in their quarters.

We medics got on well together. Mateship played a key role. Robbie was at the centre of my network of mates and worked on the surgery ward. He was totally dependable. If I was working and he wasn't, he'd bring me food, water or tea. I'd do the same for him. If one of us needed help on the ward, the other would pitch in. If one of us were ill, the other would help. This strong partnership reinforced wider partnerships with medics like Bill Graham, Ozzy Osborne (a pre-war reporter for a Brighton newspaper) and Jock Lynas, and beyond that it reinforced still wider partnerships with the whole medical unit. These relationships were arguably stronger than relationships formed at Changi and certainly were more personal.

The relationship between doctors and medics was essentially doctor/nurse rather than officer/other ranks but it varied considerably depending on the skills of the medics. Reading and writing

70

skills were uneven. But within that limitation, the relationship was good, at times close, and stronger in some respects than at Changi. The doctor-orderly relationship was founded on three elements: doctors had massive responsibilities, which required them to delegate where trust existed; experienced medics developed a good sense of what they could do and what should be left to doctors; and, in a small team, doctors and medics came to know each other very well. In my case I never really knew Lieutenant Colonel Malcolm or the microbiologist (who also was of senior rank), but I knew the others and had a good working relationship particularly with Dr Poh and the Anglo-Indian doctors. Dr Mac was prepared to discuss medical issues with me and I learnt a great deal from him. He was always the doctor I consulted whenever I was ill.

Making a difference in fighting disease: four snapshots

Dysentery
There was nothing easy about treating dysentery under the conditions prevailing at the hospital camp. A few dysentery patients were discharged from the hospital fully fit and well after a relatively brief period of discomfort. Most were discharged after showing some improvement: magnesium sulphate couldn't cure patients with bacterial dysentery. A sizeable minority lingered on in hospital for many months, reduced to living skeletons – many died; and some succumbed to devastating forms of the disease that killed them in a few weeks.

Trying to keep so many patients reasonably clean each day was next to impossible. Trying to cure them of amoebic dysentery was a dreadful business. The disease kills slowly if not treated properly with appropriate medicines, which were in very short supply. Treatment sometimes involved the surgeon, Dr de Soldinoff, doing an appendicostomy – removing the appendix and then inserting a tube into the intestines into the area where the appendix had been and keeping it there. We orderlies then had to flush out the intestines on a daily basis with a copper sulphate solution (if memory serves me), repeating this day after day, week after week. It was hard on the patients as well as on us.

My worst memory of dysentery at the hospital camp is the death of Corporal Norman Aldridge. Everything that could be done for him was done, but nothing worked against this vicious bacterial

71

form of the disease and he went from being a big, reasonably healthy bloke to something resembling a skeleton within a fortnight. Tragically, he knew precisely what was happening to him and the various stages he would pass through before death. On his final afternoon, Bill Graham was with him – they were very close – and Norman was crying out for his wife, repeating again and again his love for her and begging her for help. It was awful to hear the hopelessness and desperation in his voice. His final words were an appeal to a fellow patient and medic: 'Stick it Wally.' Wally went through an emotional hell that afternoon but he did stick it and eventually recovered.

To me, Norman's story is particularly sad because he was a friend, was fully aware of his plight and was desperate for anything that might save him. Beyond this, the story underlines our predicament as medics: if we couldn't do anything for a close friend, what could we do for others? Norman's passing made us all very fearful and raised the same old question: could this happen to me, if not today, then tomorrow or next week or next month?

Surgery: tropical ulcers

The surgical ward was the domain of Dr de Soldinoff. Everyone liked him. Bill Graham, the head orderly, ensured that the medics were up to the mark. They had to be: they did the most technically demanding work in the hospital.

The arrival of ulcer patients from mid-1943 taxed the resources of the hospital camp and the surgery ward in particular. They arrived bent double, clutching rotting legs and feet and begrimed in their own muck. Cleaning them up was the easy stage. Using chloroform to straighten their legs often came next: it was a gruesome procedure involving one medic sitting on a knee while another placed splints on the leg. Gangrenous tissue was removed and the wound treated with phenol or Lysol and a sprinkling of iodoform powder. In bad cases, amputation was the only option. Sometimes this was done right away, but usually only after other avenues had been exhausted.

The operating theatre was in the camp's central complex. The theatre had shutters in place of windows, hinged outwards to allow fresh air to circulate during operations. The theatre was draped with a large green mosquito net supplied by the Japanese and covered an area as large as a standard room. Operations were always performed during the day (usually in the afternoon) because of lighting limitations. The net, therefore, kept out flies rather than mosquitoes.

The theatre couldn't be kept sterile because of its wooden floor, the indeterminate material forming the walls and its openness to the grime and smells of the camp and surrounding farmland. The monsoon months were especially difficult. The bamboo operating table probably wasn't sterile either. The area, however, was kept clean by the theatre orderly – a bloke from Leeds who'd been with a medical headquarters unit in Singapore. He knew his business and scrubbed the place with whatever disinfectants were available. All the instruments were sterile and Dr de Soldinoff was kept sterile to the extent possible: he scrubbed up carefully, entered the theatre naked and operated in a surgical gown that had been thoroughly boiled.

I was privileged to observe some operations, including appendicectomies, and operations for throat cancer, amputations and the removal of ulcerated eyes. I wasn't part of the surgical ward but was interested in surgery and Dr de Soldinoff encouraged the interest. He sometimes described amputations as nothing more than butchery; an act of cutting meat off the bone, sawing through bone and sewing skin and flesh over stumps. Reduced to absolute basics, this might be right. But it wasn't like this in the theatre. The dental surgeon, Jimmy, sometimes assisted de Soldinoff with amputation cases. A badly ulcerated leg would be removed. Jimmy would be holding it and would place it reverently on the wooden floor. It was not just a cast-off piece of meat and bone. It had been part of a living man. It required respect.

The initial mortality rate from surgery was fairly low, around ten per cent, though around half of amputees eventually died from a combination of shock and general weakness from dysentery, malaria and avitaminosis diseases or perhaps from other complications. Those who survived were helped to recover some degree of fitness, mobility and confidence. Various forms of therapeutic massage were used to coax patients' under-used muscles back to life and strengthen remaining limbs. Light exercise groups helped to prevent further physical deterioration and improve the general fitness of moderately sick patients. Men skilled in carpentry built aids to enhance mobility or improve appearance (for example, wooden eyes). Glass eyes couldn't be manufactured at the camp, but one Dutch Javanese created highly polished wooden eyes: he must have had the patience of Job. The wooden eye kept the eye socket from shrinking so that a glass eye could be fitted later in Britain (with luck).

Cholera

The day at last arrived that we had all been dreading and hoped we might escape: someone was brought into the camp by truck with cholera. He had severe stomach pains, his legs were cramping and he was gushing so-called 'milk stools' – thin whitish material that I understand is part of the lining of the intestines being stripped away by the disease. The Japanese provided us with a small tent and we set up an isolated cholera camp about 50 yards from the dysentery ward. The tent was very hot and the flaps had to be kept open all of the time. We erected a barbed wire fence around the tent. The Japanese supplied the barbed wire but wouldn't go near the camp.

Once the first dreadful shock was over, the outbreak didn't have a major impact on the hospital. Some of the blokes in the nearby dysentery ward were so sick they probably weren't overly concerned by the news. Those who were less sick worried, as we did, but eventually we all stoically accepted it. Dr Poh and Dr Mac attended the patient once or more each day, and I was one of three orderlies who nursed him in roughly eight-hour shifts. There were no volunteers from the infantry or elsewhere for this work. Who could blame them? We gave the bloke a paste of glycerine and potassium permanganate in pill form. He swallowed the pills with difficulty but there was no discernible benefit. We tried to get fluid into him. He should have had an intravenous saline drip but we didn't have the equipment and didn't think of making a Heath Robinson substitute. We just never got enough fluid into him through slow sipping and he shrank and shrivelled before our eyes. You saw the bones appearing and the skin wrinkling. You could pinch his skin and it would stick up and stay that way.

We didn't have rubber gloves or other aids like face masks. The milk stools inevitably got on our hands and there was always a danger of touching the mouth in a moment of carelessness. I kept plunging my hands into a very strong disinfectant supplied by the Japanese. It skinned them but this was a small price to pay. Before going back to the wards or to bed, I washed meticulously in disinfectant. Like the other medics and doctors, I wore only a loincloth,

74

which was boiled after each shift. It was critical to avoid an epidemic and we hoped to survive.

The poor fellow died after less than a week. We burnt the body. The Japanese allowed us to gather wood for the funeral pyre but required the cremation to take place outside the hospital camp and well away from the guardroom at the camp's entrance. They also insisted that the body could not be brought past the guardroom and authorised opening part of the perimeter fence, which wasn't difficult because it was so flimsy. Burning the body was a horrible task, made slightly easier because some of us had watched Thai and Chinese funerals at Ban Pong. The worst part was ensuring that the whole body burnt evenly because this doesn't happen by chance. To do this we had to keep poking the body with long sticks. You didn't want a head rolling around, so we kept poking. It was horrible to think this had been a human being. It was a traumatic experience and came with only one benefit, at least for me. The Korean guard who'd been pursuing me around the camp for some misdemeanour on my part stopped doing so because I was the 'cholera man'. He and the other guards didn't want me anywhere near them. That suited me fine.

Everyone dreaded another cholera case being brought into the hospital camp or, worse still, an epidemic within the camp through the contamination of the water supply. Cholera continued to lurk in the general area. There were ongoing cases at Tarsau and a case at Chungkai in early 1944, by which time the hospital camp had closed. At the Kanchanaburi Aerodrome Camp, our next rotation, we were able to respond to the threat with Japanese-supplied cholera vaccine. This was a massive advance on the Japanese injunction a few months earlier at the hospital camp for each person to kill a daily quota of flies.

Food as medicine

With so few medicines available, men's lives often balanced precariously on access to small additional quantities of nutritious foods. The most spectacular example of this that I saw was a patient suffering from wet beriberi. The swelling crept up his body and he ballooned eventually from head to foot: his tongue was grotesquely swollen and he had one fit after another as the swelling reached his brain. We fed him the hospital's last jar of Marmite. It saved him. He'd been so close to dying. For days he did nothing but pass water.

It flooded out of him. The swelling went down and he returned to his half-starved normal self within a week or so. His recovery would have made an excellent advertisement for the rich vitamin B content of Marmite. But using this last jar to save a life left the hospital with a problem: how to deal with extremely bad cases of avitaminosis in the future? Without Marmite, we could use rice polishings, but they were slower acting and not as effective. They wouldn't have saved someone who'd experienced seventeen fits in one night.

A less spectacular example was the hospital's special diets programme. From March 1943 to the end of the year when the camp closed, part of my morning ritual was to meet an old Thai man at the guardroom to receive supplies of liver, soy milk and duck eggs. The quantities were quite small. The liver might serve half a dozen patients, there might be a dozen or so eggs and a pint or two of soy milk. It was always more or less the same food in the same small quantities. Johnny Bull was the cook who prepared the liver in a special area that was separate from the cookhouse. He looked like a Hollywood rogue with his darkish good looks, sideburns and moustache, but was straightforward and honest. I fed the cooked liver, soy milk and hard-boiled eggs to the neediest patients as identified by the doctors. It helped to keep some desperately sick men going who might otherwise have had no chance of survival, though some were too sick to digest the liver and lost any benefit by vomiting the lot.

The special diets programme demonstrates some of the strengths of POW society. The food wasn't free. Around 200 officers at the camp and in the surrounding area contributed part of their 'wages' to the hospital to buy additional food and medicine. The Red Cross, and maybe even the Thai resistance, contributed. Also, starving men were trusted to have the self-discipline to provide nourishment to those in greatest need.

Making a difference in death

Like many others, I saw helping dying men as a duty and I tried to stay with them for as long as I could. No one could change anything. No one could bring blokes back because they'd slipped too far.

In the last few days of life, many patients still realise what is happening to them, are terribly afraid and often lonely. Some would show you creased photographs from their wallets of happy faces in better times. You'd look at the young bloke on the sleeping platform and the person in the photograph: the resemblance might no longer exist. They'd reminisce about their pasts, talk about their families and how much they wanted to go home, and you knew they never would. That was all they wanted to talk about. Poor lads: they were thousands of miles away from their families, and those families in all likelihood would never know the precise circumstances of a loved one's passing. They would have to deal with grief in any way they could. Offering some care and compassion was the least we could do, but it was never enough in wards where there were many scores of very sick men. The hospital camp's Roman Catholic padre was invaluable in sharing this load. He was such a kind and compassionate man and so focused on the message of Jesus Christ. For a lad with a strong, and perhaps bigoted, evangelical upbringing, he changed my views permanently about Catholics.

In their final hours, patients are often semi-conscious, don't know where they are and barely speak. It takes all their effort to breath. It is pitiful. But it was important for them to know, however vaguely, that someone was with them. We tried to make them more comfortable by getting the bedding right, sponging them down because they were often very hot, and swabbing their mouths with glycerine to improve the taste and add moisture and 'softness'. Water wasn't anywhere near as good. Regrettably, many slipped away without any of these comforts. You'd go around the ward, particularly at night, and see them in the light of a little oil lamp. There were sometimes so many of them. They'd be taken from the ward. Death would be confirmed and then they'd be prepared for burial in the morning. It was all very mechanical.

I'm sure doctors and medics never really got used to all this death. We shared part of a wretched journey with our patients. What we did wasn't hopeless or futile, even without adequate medicines. We did our best. We weren't often overwhelmed by the injustice of it all or by our impotence to change outcomes in so many cases. We made a difference and fate took care of the rest. The collective strength of the team, and especially the leadership of doctors, was paramount in staying focused.

All this death inevitably made you harder, or just more realistic, but it was important that it didn't make you indifferent or callous, as it so easily could. Inevitably there were examples of indifference. An image comes to mind of two orderlies and two volunteers playing cards next to a dying man who was gasping for breath. But there weren't many examples of wilful neglect. Doctors, orderlies and volunteers did their level best every day to help patients within the restrictions dictated by adverse circumstances.

Closing the hospital camp

Towards the end of the 1943, rumours started to circulate that the hospital camp was about to close. On this occasion they were correct. The hospital was functioning as well as it ever had and the buildings were in good repair, but Japanese priorities had changed in the post-railway building phase. Most of the 'railway men' were being sent back to southern Thailand (mainly to the Kanchanaburi area) to work on various projects like servicing the operational requirements of the railway. Some returned to Singapore; others went to Japan and a few to Indo-China. The hospital was surplus to requirements. Patients left the hospital camp by mid-December 1943. Most were moved to hospitals further downriver. The medical staff was scattered, but many medics, including me, were reassigned to the Kanchanaburi Aerodrome Camp – one of the many work camps in the area.

I look back at the hospital camp with mixed feelings. The camp was successful within the strictures of its inadequate resourcing: it held together by combining skills and through hard work for the common good. Without this cohesion and sense of purpose, the human toll would have been so much greater. I also learnt a great deal at the camp. I observed several operations. I learnt more about dysentery and malaria from Dr Mac. I learnt about diet and therapeutic massage. I also learnt to play bridge well. But basically I was glad the camp was closing. It wasn't a pleasant place. There was hunger and privation. Disease was rampant. There was pointless and unnecessary death because of the half rations and scarcity of medicines. It was difficult to survive there, though medical staff kept reasonably fit on the whole. And there was never enough time for the large number of patients. Patient care probably deteriorated over the year, especially from mid-1943. Blokes were packed in like sardines in a tin.

I was delighted when I found out that my next rotation would be the Kanchanaburi Aerodrome Camp. The prospect of little disease and full rations was very attractive.

Chapter 7

Glimpses of 'King Rat'

The Kanchanaburi Aerodrome Camp was a short distance away from the abandoned hospital camp and was sited where Amy Johnson landed her de Havilland Gipsy Moth en route to Alor Setar in north Malaya and eventually Australia in May 1930. The town of Kanchanaburi could just be seen from the camp and the hooter on the town's paper mill could be heard clearly at midday.

This large work camp was set up for 'fit' men who worked on projects in the surrounding region, including Japanese camps. The work wasn't especially gruelling and was sometimes pleasant. We had time off, could make money on the side through a reasonably large-scale cigarette business and buy additional food. The deal making and good living provide faint glimpses of the title character – minus the control, manipulation, meanness and fine clothes – in James Clavell's 1962 novel *King Rat*, which is set during the Second World War in Changi. We also weren't constantly harassed by violent guards. Some guards were surprisingly decent. Camp discipline could be severe – the camp commandant, for example, had two Geordies put down a water-filled hole for three weeks, allowing them one ball of rice per day and a bottle of water, for stealing something he regarded as sensitive. But, by and large, it wasn't difficult to survive at the camp.

Most medical orderlies and some doctors from the hospital camp were assigned initially to the aerodrome camp, joining prisoners from up-country work camps who were no longer needed on the railway. The small camp hospital had about 100 'light sick' patients and was run by Major de Soldinoff and Captain Jim Marks. Diseases like beriberi and pellagra existed in a minor way because we received full rations. It was still rice and vegetable stew, but there was much more of it and we didn't have hunger pangs all of the time. Dysentery and malaria were under control.

No one expected patient numbers to surge and the hospital already had a full complement of medical orderlies. Some hospital camp medics were reassigned to other camps, including in Japan, and the rest of us were assigned to non-medical work. My pal Robbie was among those reassigned to other camps. I told Robbie I'd volunteer to go with him. He discouraged me, mentioning the old adage about never volunteering for anything in the Army. That advice probably saved my life. A large working party was sent to Japan around this time. The rumour mill suggested that the convoy was attacked by US submarines and many POWs were killed. I never heard from Robbie again.

Working parties

It's hard dealing with the loss of someone as close as a brother. Not having a best mate also made me feel vulnerable, even though I was among friends and there were several hundred blokes within a stone's throw. Sid Browne, from Norwich, was in the Field Ambulance and was in a similar position to me: his best mate had just been drafted to another camp. Sid suggested we team up and I readily agreed. He was a fine, dependable man. I moved over to a sleeping platform near him, Sammy Robinson (a bloke from near Halifax), Iggy (from Lancashire), Nighty (from Norfolk) and Proudlove (a Regular Soldier from the South of England). We got on like a house on fire.

I spent about seven months away from medical work on various working parties. For the most part we weren't doing physically demanding work and sometimes it was easy. Being out most days also provided a wonderful opportunity to pick fruit – papayas, pomegranates, bananas, passion fruit, and pumpkins – at abandoned *kampongs* or on land that wasn't being tended carefully. That made a difference: fruit could be shared with mates and friends back at camp. I can understand why some blokes from up-country work camps remember Kanchanaburi as a place for fattening-up. We didn't get fat at the aerodrome camp – there were always blokes eating their meals in the 'legge', or leftovers queue, anxiously looking for scraps – but we didn't face slow starvation on half rations as we did at the hospital camp.

Our jobs were all labouring and were good or bad depending on the guards in charge. Some appalling characters from the hospital camp, like the Undertaker, were transferred to the aerodrome camp.

Barked orders, misunderstood and hesitant responses, face slapping, and occasional spirited beatings were standard features of their working parties. Having an effective British or Aussie officer on hand was so important in those circumstances. An officer did a good job if he could interpret, more or less, the job specifications and became the buffer between the guards and us. Our officers were generally very good. The officer I came in contact with most was a young guy, only a year or two older than most of us. He faced angry tirades and was knocked about on occasions, but he stood his ground. He didn't do any manual work but more than did his duty.

I was lucky to be taken out only once by the Undertaker. Our party went into the forest to collect small trees – the commandant wanted to soften the appearance of the camp by planting trees and shrubs along its main 'avenues'. The Undertaker developed malaria, had a roaring temperature and was shaking like a leaf. Like well-trained schoolboys we collected a few plants and took off early back to camp. Some blokes half carried him and I shouldered his rifle. When we returned, guards swarmed out of the guardroom, grabbed the rifle and questioned us, quickly realising that the Undertaker was very sick.

I also was lucky to avoid the Japanese *gunso* most of the time. He was another mean bastard and you walked on eggshells in his presence. He was rumoured to be a syphilitic on account of his mad and violent behaviour. He took pleasure in kicking blokes hard in the shins if they didn't stand properly to attention (as defined by him), throwing stones at our officers and beating prisoners and Korean guards alike for whimsical reasons. It might be a look or an on-the-spot decision not to suffer you. On one occasion he nearly killed a Korean guard who had the misfortune to land a blow while being instructed in one of the martial arts.

Most jobs in the Japanese camps were of the make-work type, like sweeping up, and there was a good deal of hanging about as guards thought up something to occupy us. Occasionally, spiteful guards invented ways to make simple jobs quite disgusting. One was cleaning out the stables of twenty or so sick ponies. They had wide canvass bands around their stomachs and were suspended slightly from the rafters so they didn't fall over. Cleaning out the stables wouldn't have been onerous except that the guards decided we didn't need shovels and could use our hands to shovel the muck into bamboo skips before disposing of it in the latrines. I dread to think what would have happened if those ponies had been suffering from serious diseases and the infection had been passed to us through cuts or abrasions on our hands, arms or legs because the muck got everywhere. There never was much danger of ingesting it by touching our mouths. Fortunately no harm came from the experience, though the ponies gave one or two blokes solid kicks for their efforts.

A sizeable minority of guards were decent enough. They didn't get tough or ill treat us in order to achieve the results they wanted. There were moments, sometimes lengthy periods, when life was relatively good. My first job was working in a large vegetable garden belonging to a Japanese ordnance (military supplies) unit. The garden was close to the River Kwai and growing conditions were excellent. I spent most days planting and watering. It was pleasant work with regular breaks, including swimming. The river was fast-flowing even in the dry season. As you swam across it, the opposite bank flashed past as the current took hold of you. It was great exercise marred only by the *Kempeitai* – secret police – headquarters on the opposite bank from the garden. I never saw any prisoners but I occasionally heard men and women screaming. It was frightening.

A Japanese private from the ordnance unit supervised us for a time. He was a thoroughly reasonable man. There were no cross words and, most importantly, he stopped the bullying tactics of the Korean guards. He even gave us *sake* on his birthday. He drank a lot that day and was so happy. Other ordnance fellows were decent too, though we didn't see them much. Some showed us photographs of their families. They talked about how much they wanted the war to be over so they could return home. We talked about our families and hopes. Language wasn't much of barrier: they knew some English, we knew some Japanese, and the flow of conversation was smoothed by cups of green tea and the rice biscuits they shared with us. They were engaging people.

On another occasion, a large group of us was assigned for a week or two to help construct the camp commandant's new house. It was a beautiful house overlooking the river. A Japanese private – we called him Christian Charlie – was in charge of the project. He was a qualified joiner who worked across the camps in the Kanchanaburi area: I first came across him when he was building new wards at the hospital camp. He was reasonable, honest and fair. In his broken

English he explained how he wanted as many prisoners as possible to receive full pay and rations, so he always took out many more men than he needed on working parties. He said this was the Christian thing to do, adding that he expected steady work and prisoners to look busy when Japanese officers came on inspection tours. Bags of soft nails were kept handy for such occasions: parts of the supports of the house must have been covered in nails, so spirited was the hammering during inspections. Charlie wasn't a slave driver and blokes responded positively to him.

Around mid-1944, we were assigned to a Japanese camp to dig concealment trenches for trucks. Increased Allied bombing was making this more urgent. Prisoners were split up among groups of Japanese soldiers. It was back-breaking work. On one occasion I ended up with a group headed by a sergeant major and including some *gunsos*. They were jovial as they dug away and I tried to keep up with them. The sergeant major called '*yasme*' – a smoking break – and they all stopped while I kept on going. He came over to me, put his hand on my shoulder and said '*yasme*'. He then poured me a cup of tea and offered rice biscuits. This amazed me: a man of his rank offering me tea and biscuits. I expected him to treat me like dirt but instead he was decent and friendly. He probably wanted to go home just as much as I did. After half an hour we resumed work.

We spent some weeks cutting bamboo under the supervision of Korean guards, each day walking several miles along the River Kwai before crossing the railway line, where the concrete and steel bridge at Tamarkan started, to begin the day's work. At times it could be very strenuous. Our axes were blunt and hauling cut bamboo from tangled undergrowth was never easy. There also were some risks. You could hit the base of a bamboo and the axe might spring off. Thin bamboos could split and deliver nasty wounds. Red ants and bush bees could be problems – I was stung badly on the face on one occasion – and I was struck by a snake on the finger. I don't know what it was but my arm started to swell and a lump formed under my armpit. I cleared off as fast as I could to the Medical Inspection Room at the camp for attention. But, as jobs go, cutting bamboo wasn't bad providing there were reasonable guards.

By far the best guard was a Korean we called 'Joey'. We could relate to him as a person. He was small, pleasant and good-natured. He allowed us to buy tobacco and food from market stalls and, above all, was flexible and practical in negotiating output quotas.

We struck an agreement that each man would cut twenty bamboos of a certain size each day and that the bamboos would then be parcelled together and loaded onto trucks. This benefitted both parties. Joey achieved a high level of output that satisfied his bosses and we took off the rest of the day.

Joey was joined occasionally by another Korean guard we called 'Tab End'. He was always searching for cigarette ends on hut floors or stuck in the ends of bamboo sleeping platforms and beating up blokes suspected of littering. We expected the worst when he joined the working party but discovered that his personality changed completely outside the camp. He became pleasantly normal, which made us think the 'hard man' approach in camp was a mask to please elements of the Japanese military. Whatever it was, towards the end of 1944 he approached Bill Graham with an escape proposal: he would get them through the Japanese lines if Bill could get them through the British lines. Bill refused, thinking it was a set-up. The following day, the *Kempeitai* arrested Tab End. We never saw him again.

We spent a couple of weeks demolishing huts at the old hospital camp under the direction of a Korean guard. He was obsessed with washing his hands and was increasingly introspective. In the end he didn't speak to anyone or issue orders, so the demolition work proceeded on our own initiative. One day the guard disappeared and the working party marched back to camp at the appointed time without him. Guards searched the hospital camp and discovered he'd shot himself.

Looking back at these months in the first half of 1944, I was fortunate that some of my jobs were congenial and supervised by reasonable fellows, both Japanese and Korean. We still had more than our fair share of awkward or violent guards and were still stuck in a situation that seemed to be unending, but the work was less intense and demanding than at the hospital camp. There was a life beyond work that embraced the occasional concert; making grog from a noxious and heady mixture of yeast, sweet potato peelings, sugar and water; playing bridge; and exploring the surrounding countryside with its myriad shades of green, profusion of brightly coloured wildlife and abundant fruit. We also had time to build up our cigarette racket – the best way a small group of us ever devised to make money to buy extra food.

Our wedding day. Marion and me at Bar Chapel, Harrogate. (*Author's collection*)

Marion and baby Diane. (*Author's collection*)

Marion and me with our best man, my brother-in-law Harry Jackson, and matron of honour, my sister Betty. (*Author's collection*)

The West Yorkshire Road Car Company. The company gave me my first job after leaving school. (*North Yorks County Council*)

The Air Ministry at Harlow Manor – Marion's wartime employer. (*North Yorks County Council*)

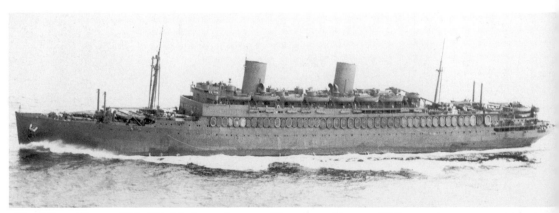

The *Mount Vernon*. This US ship brought me to Singapore, January 1942. (*Australian War Memorial 303655*)

Murray Griffin's painting of an Australian advanced dressing station near Tengah Airfield, Singapore, February 1942. The RAMC operated along similar lines. (*Australian War Memorial ART24478*)

First aid helpers carrying wounded after an air raid in Singapore, early February 1942. (*Australian War Memorial 011529/15*)

Victorious Japanese soldiers on the Singapore Waterfront, 16 February 1942.
(*Australian War Memorial 127905*)

Murray Griffin's painting of part of a ward at Roberts Hospital, Changi POW Camp. The painting was conceived in early 1942 and completed the following year. Note the bed sheets – keeping them relatively clean was a nightmare, particularly in a dysentery ward. After a few weeks, sheets were abandoned.
(*Australian War Memorial ART24478*)

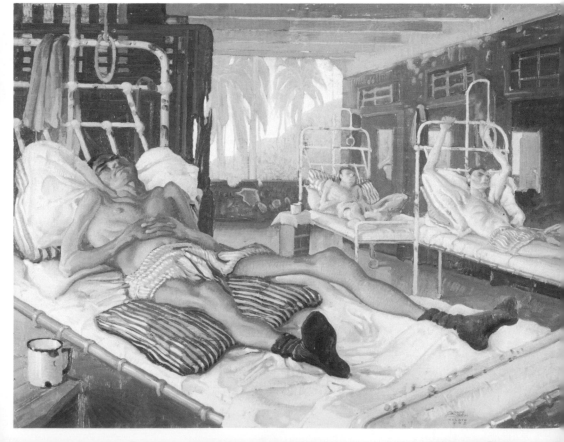

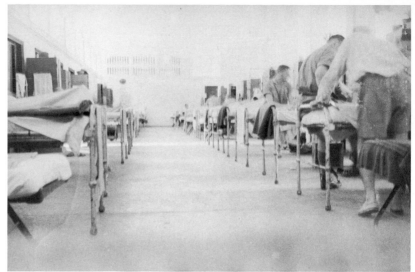

Doctors and medics attending patients at Roberts Hospital, Changi POW Camp. The photograph was taken shortly after the hospital opened. Photographs were taken secretly and at great risk to all concerned. (*Australian War Memorial PO4485.049*)

View from one of the upstairs windows at Roberts Hospital, Changi POW Camp. (*Australian War Memorial PO4485.073*)

Gardening at Roberts Hospital. Gardens provided essential additional food. (*Australian War Memorial PO4485.006*)

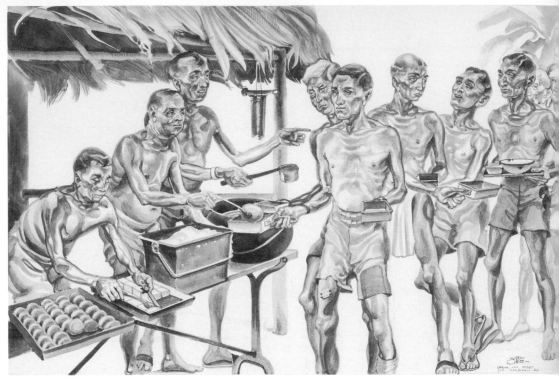

Queuing at the cookhouse, Changi POW Camp. Rice was provided by the Japanese. We watched like hawks to see that it was divided equally. (*Australian War Memorial ART25102*)

Selarang Barracks Square Incident. For three days in early September 1942, around 16,000 British and Australian POWs were held in increasingly foul conditions until they agreed to sign no-escape undertakings. (*Australian War Memorial 123940*)

Steel carriages similar to those used to transport POWs from Singapore to Thailand. Around forty men were packed into each carriage. (*Australian War Memorial 157866*)

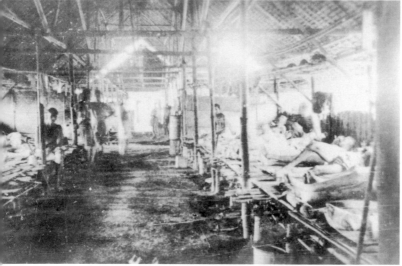

Interior of a British medical ward at the Kanchanaburi Hospital Camp. (*Australian War Memorial P01433.018*)

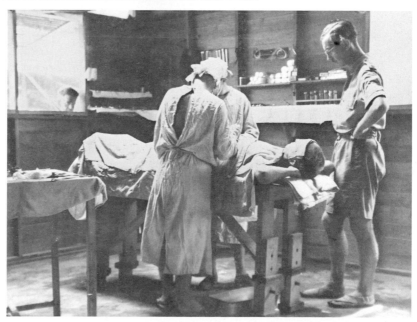

Surgery at the Hospital Camp's operating theatre. (*Australian War Memorial 157874*)

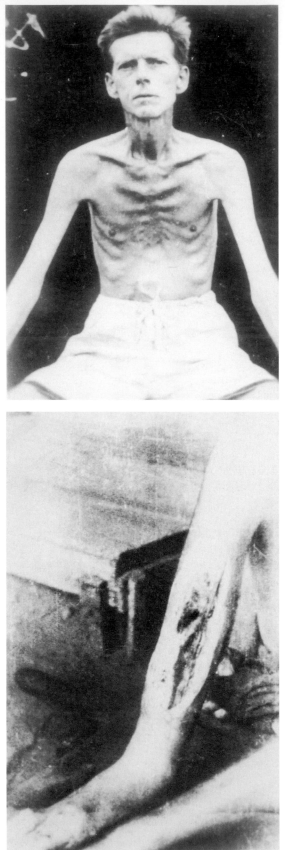

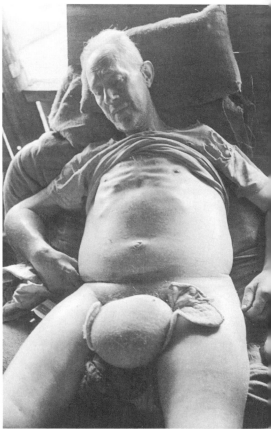

An emaciated POW suffering from dysentery. (*Australian War Memorial P01433.022*)

A POW suffering from beriberi and arterial sclerosis. (*Australian War Memorial 030362/05*)

An advanced tropical leg ulcer. Large numbers of ulcer patients were brought to the Kanchanaburi Hospital Camp, some in a desperate state, from mid-1943. (*Australian War Memorial P00761.010*)

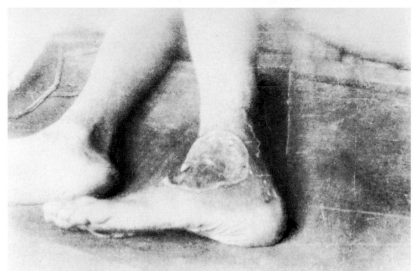

A tropical ulcer on a POW's ankle. (*Australian War Memorial P00761.009*)

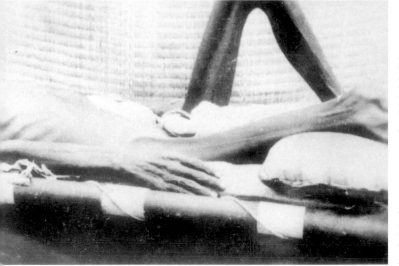

A shrunken cholera victim in one of the base hospitals. Cholera was a problem, especially in the wet season. (*Australian War Memorial P01433.027*)

Typical attap huts at the Kanchanaburi POW Camp. (*Australian War Memorial P01502.008*)

A typical interior of an open-sided attap hut at the Kanchanaburi POW Camp.
(*Australian War Memorial P01502.006*)

The meal queue at one of the Kanchanaburi canteens, January 1945. (*Australian War Memorial 1502.007*)

A POW urinal. (*Australian War Memorial 157869*)

A POW punishment hole. (*Australian War Memorial 157872*)

High-sided barges like those used to transport us from the Kanchanaburi POW Camp to the Taimuang Camp and later, to Bangkok.
(*Australian War Memorial P00406.013*)

A typical POW hut under construction at the Taimuang POW Camp.
(*Australian War Memorial P01433.012*)

A bullock cart like the one we pulled for part of the way between Nakhon Nayok, in eastern Thailand, to Phitsanulok, in north central Thailand, during the final months of the war. Among other things, the cart carried rice supplies and sometimes POWs who were too weak to march.
(*Author's collection*)

Miracle of freedom: the food supply improved overnight. (*Australian War Memorial 157880*)

A Dakota bringing former POWs from Thailand to the Mingaladon Airstrip, Rangoon. (*Australian War Memorial SUK14683*)

SS *Chitral* – the ship that brought me home. This photograph was taken in July 1946, when the *Chitral* was in Kure, Japan, about to repatriate New Zealand troops. (*Australian War Memorial 130250*)

Bomb damage in Leeds: houses destroyed on Rosemount View, March 1941. Attacks were especially severe at this time and resulted in significant loss of life and property damage. The damage was quickly repaired. (*Leodis*)

Bomb damage in Leeds: Model Road after the March 1941 air raids. Note the air raid shelter built in the road. (*Leodis*)

Leeds City Centre, October 1944. There is no evidence of extensive bomb damage, which is one of the reasons why I felt so much at home there. (*Leodis*)

Parliament Street, in early post-war Harrogate. The town was virtually untouched by bombing. (*Unnetie*)

James Street, in early post-war Harrogate. (*Unnetie*)

The Royal Hall, 1946.
(*Unnetie*)

The children's pool at
the Valley Gardens,
1948. (*Unnetie*)

My family: Marion,
Diane and Michael,
1948. (*Author's collection*)

The cigarette racket

The cigarette racket started shortly after we arrived at the aero-drome camp and continued through to mid-1944 when the Japanese commandant closed it down. I proposed launching the racket as a means to an end: more income meant more food and more food increased the chances of surviving. The market for cigarettes was huge: concerns about the effects of smoking were all in the future and, frankly, wouldn't have made any difference even if they'd been known. Smoking offered comfort and deadened hunger pains. The business challenge, therefore, was the age-old one: how to bring a quality product to market at a competitive price?

I went around all the medics in our hut asking if blokes would risk one month's wages for seed capital. It was asking a lot. It meant not buying eggs or cigarettes for what seemed like a long time. Only five friends, Sid Browne, Sammy, Iggy, Nighty and Proudlove, were prepared to do this, probably because we were close mates. We christened our business the Rich and Mild Company (RAMC), the acronym resonating because we were all members of the Royal Army Medical Corps. Almost immediately we went on a shopping spree with the seed capital. We bought two cigarette-rolling machines from blokes in the camp. The machines were nothing special, just wood and canvas, but we paid through the nose for them. We also invested in catties, 18 inches long by 12 inches wide and about 2 inches thick, of strong black Thai tobacco called Sikh's Beard. It was terrible stuff. It nearly choked you and blinded you with tears until you got used to it.

By the light of little oil lamps made from tin cans, we rolled about 400 cigarettes on the first night of our business enterprise before realising a major flaw in our plans. We were launching a business based potentially on scale and division of labour principles and were expecting the market to come to us. It didn't, of course. Dr de Soldinoff solved the marketing problem. He sent for me and said he might be able to get orders from other camps drawing on his wider medical contacts. Next day he announced an order for 500 cigarettes per day. That got us going and provided the found-ation for all our subsequent work to develop a good product for the market.

We initially used pages torn from the Bible for cigarette paper. The padre told us that quarrying the Bible was acceptable so long as blokes read every word on those papers before smoking them. The

85

injunction was probably more honoured in the breach. After about two weeks, we substituted Thai cigarette paper. It was expensive and mostly of indifferent quality, but it improved the look and taste of our cigarettes and removed residual ethical doubts. We also tried washing and drying the tobacco to make it less acrid but it then tasted like straw so we abandoned the experiment. More orders came in from other camps, arranged for us by blokes on the various working parties and by truck drivers for the Japanese who had excellent contacts. They all worked on a commission basis.

About this time, we started to sell cigarettes within the aerodrome camp. The business grew strongly. We sold more and more standard cigarettes made with Thai tobacco and started making Virginia cigarettes using superior papers. The Virginia line sold very well, particularly among officers. We found a printing set and printed RAMC on each Virginia cigarette, perhaps anticipating a time when branded identity and product differentiation would become important. We never considered producing filter-tipped cigarettes. Finding filters would have been a nightmare.

To meet demand, our average daily production rose quickly from 500 to 1,000 and then to 1,500, before stabilising at a little over 2,000. Maintaining this was demanding because we only had evenings and weekends. The weekend was observed at the camp at this time, which was a big change from the hospital camp. Weekend production naturally increased because we rolled and packed cigarettes from morning till night. The more we produced, the more we kept ahead of our orders. We were keen to consolidate our emerging reputation for quality and reliability.

It was hard work. Production had to be fast but quality control required meeting a uniform standard. By and large Sammy and Iggy were the rollers, Nighty pasted the cigarette papers with tapioca flour, and Sid straightened the cigarette ends – off-cuts were used for our line in pipe tobacco – and packed the finished product in groups of ten. I assisted Sid and looked after the 'books' – the one cashbook – and our working capital, which was stashed in our hut's attap roof. The money was quite safe. We were all medics at our end of the hut and there was always someone there. Proudlove was the chief salesman. He received orders from around the camp and kept meticulous records of those buying on credit. He had an amazing capacity to chase up debts, even from among the officers.

The production line required tobacco, which had to be smuggled into camp past the guards. Smuggling was a risky business. Smugglers had to be cunning and expected to be well rewarded. A common ploy was stuffing tobacco into cooking pots used to prepare lunchtime meals, but each smuggler had his favourite concealment tricks.

The rapid growth and scale of our business undercut other suppliers at the camp. They were generally blokes who'd made or invested in a rolling machine and worked by themselves. After a few weeks of intensified competition, they claimed they couldn't make money and proposed raising prices across the board by ten per cent. This was agreed. I asked Proudlove to confirm that all parties were honouring the agreement. They weren't. Competitors were selling at the old price. I called a meeting of all suppliers and proposed two alternatives: RAMC could reduce prices by ten per cent and ruin their businesses or RAMC could agree to buy all their production at the normal retail price providing it met our quality standards. The second option was agreed and increased our capacity to respond to growing demand. By this time we supplied almost all of the aerodrome camp's cigarette requirements and a good part of neighbouring camps' requirements too.

This was big business for us. We probably quadrupled our wages after paying suppliers and contractors, holding back money for contingencies and donating each Friday night's rolling to the lads in hospital, who received around twenty cigarettes each. There was no pressure to do this, unlike at some other camps. At Tamarkan, for example, there was a requirement to contribute ten per cent of cigarette racket profits to the hospital fund. Our voluntary approach was superior. It made a larger contribution to the hospital because ten per cent of our profits wouldn't have added up to much. The lads appreciated the cigarettes and the gesture was welcomed by the doctors and the rest of the camp. We could have bought fruit, which would be acceptable nowadays, but the lads wanted cigarettes.

After having very little money for so long, it was wonderful to be comparatively wealthy. It might have been only $30 per month each, but it went a long way and was substantial when compared to a private's standard wage of twenty-five cents per day and the even lower wage received by medics. The Japanese connived to pay us less on the grounds that the Imperial Japanese Army wasn't obligated to make up an alleged shortfall in Red Cross funding. I could now buy things like eggs on rice biscuits and 'coffee' at the canteen, and marvellous cooked dishes at local markets. There was little or no opportunity to buy meat. I only ever bought food. There was nothing else I wanted. Other members of the 'board' did the same.

Good times have a habit of coming to an end and that was the case with our business. After about five months, profits started to fall for reasons beyond our control. A vital part of the business was smuggling catties of tobacco into the camp using blokes on working parties. Unfortunately, all outside working parties from the aerodrome camp were temporarily suspended for unexplained reasons for a few weeks around May or June 1944. This meant we had to hire blokes from the camp next door to buy tobacco and take the risk of passing it to us through a gap in the fence. Guards were constantly patrolling this area to enforce a no fraternisation policy. The risks were real – being beaten up was no trivial matter – and the extra payments to those willing to take the risks were substantial. We could have raised our prices to cover the additional costs but it wouldn't have been fair on the blokes and was never considered seriously. By mid-year, profits had been slashed by more than half, but this still left enough to buy significant amounts of food.

The success of our business, even during the phase of steeply falling profits, created tensions. Some medics, who had refused to contribute seed money for the venture, now wanted to share the benefits. We never had a problem sharing additional food with a wider group of friends, but we had a problem with those who claimed, like one quartermaster sergeant, that the racket should now benefit all medics. Frankly, we saw this criticism as an enormous cheek because that had been the original proposal – for medics to run a business for everyone's benefit. The criticism was irritating but manageable. What turned out to be unmanageable was opposition from the Chinese who ran the camp's canteen. The success of our enterprise cut into their profits. They were operating on slender margins and they complained loudly.

The racket ended after the British commandant passed on an order from the Japanese commandant that the racket must be terminated immediately. We were warned of the penalties for continuing in the face of an explicit instruction to stop. We didn't need any convincing. Around this time we'd seen what had happened to a Scottish bloke who'd persisted with a 'coffee' racket. He'd been beaten savagely in the guardroom and then hauled off by the

Kempeitai, emerging six weeks later from their Kanchanaburi head-quarters a shadow of his former self. His emaciated body and staring, terrified eyes told us all we needed to know. The bastards must have put him through hell. We promptly sold off our tobacco and ceased to trade. The business was wound up around July 1944.

I have no idea why the Chinese at the canteen were so effective in closing us down. The guards generally treated them with contempt and loathing. Perhaps some were providing 'protection services' and receiving part of the canteen's profits, but the guards were predominantly Koreans and their views would have had no influence on the Japanese commandant. It beggars belief that the commandant could have been beholden to the Chinese for a few extra dollars a month. I think the decision to close us down was based on concerns that the racket was substantial, fostered links with neighbouring camps and, however improbably, posed security risks at a time when British forces were making headway in Burma and Allied planes were a growing and menacing presence.

Ending production was unfortunate in several ways. We had supplied quality cigarettes to a large number of blokes in several camps, including lads in hospital, and the business had made a big difference to our incomes. Going back to basic pay was a terrible blow. In the past, when we hadn't much money, we grudgingly accepted our low income as a fact of life. Once we'd enjoyed the benefits of money, those same facts of life seemed very unfair, at least for a while until we readjusted to penury.

The Medical Inspection (MI) Room
Around July 1944, the aerodrome camp went through one of the regular cycles of change and review that seemed to be a feature of camps in southern Thailand and maybe elsewhere. Some prisoners were sent to other camps. Others were assigned to different huts. A bunch of us were assigned to a hut that was closer to the hospital and functioned partly as the MI room – a type of medical day centre treating a range of commonplace maladies. Dr de Soldinoff asked me to run the room, the medic who'd previously done this having been transferred to another camp. It was a change from the working parties and I much preferred medical work.

It was the best job I ever had as a POW. My boss, Dr Jim Marks, was an easygoing, overworked doctor from Northern Ireland and was excellent to work with. There was variety in the day, good contact with a broad range of people and, within reason, an opportunity to build up medical expertise through trial and error. In a small way it was like being a general practitioner and I approached the job as if this was going to be my way of life.

There were three parts to a typical day as the MI room medic: a busy period early in the morning centred on the 8.00 am sick parade; a quiet period during the rest of the morning and afternoon; and a hectic period following the 8.00 pm sick parade.

The morning parade always produced dramas if the number of fit blokes available for working parties fell below whatever numbers the Japanese required. The guards wanted almost everyone to work and Dr Marks, who normally took sick parades, had to decide who was fit to work and who wasn't. Depending on which guards were present, he came in for much verbal abuse but remained adamant that men with dysentery and malaria couldn't work. The monsoons always brought more malaria because of the upsurge in the mosquito population and more dysentery because of the difficulty of maintaining adequate hygiene while sloshing around in ankle-deep mud. Some guards accepted these facts only after lengthy bickering about the extent of prisoners' incapacities: did twenty motions or less a day enable you to work?

After the sick parade and the flurry of follow-up activity, the rest of the morning and afternoon was fairly quiet. An hour or two would pass pleasantly chatting to patients in the hospital and to whoever was around the camp. British, American and Aussie prisoners would occasionally drop into the MI room for a chat. Chatting to some of the big Aussies from the bush was particularly enjoyable. They were always rattling on about the virtues of the bush – 'You can't be an Aussie and come from Sydney or Melbourne' – and were so refreshingly practical. They could put their hands to anything and got on with things while we waited for orders. I remember one chap suggesting quite seriously that a group of us should go to Australia after the war, pool our gratuities and build a business. With so many practical people to guide it, the business might have done very well.

The rest of the morning and afternoon was usually spent cleaning cuts and abrasions, dressing wounds, changing dressings, and treating skin and ear infections. It wasn't onerous work. Men on working parties inevitably cut and bruised themselves chopping bamboo and building or demolishing huts. Bamboo can be dangerous. The side

90

branches have to be removed first. They are razor-sharp and inflict nasty wounds if concentration wavers. Blokes would wash minor wounds and leave the rest to nature: there was little or no danger of cuts turning into tropical ulcers in the Kanchanaburi region and there were no ulcer cases at the small hospital. More serious cuts were treated with a mild antiseptic and might have to be stitched.

Treating skin and ear infections was a big part of MI room work. A bloke nicknamed 'Tinea' had tried and failed to find a cure for the skin infection in camps across southern Thailand. He was desperate because the infection had spread across his body and he was being shunned because no one wanted to risk getting a bad infection. I told Tinea I'd treat him at his own risk. He agreed. I remembered Dr Marks using formalin successfully on skin rashes and applied a mixture of formalin and a sulphur solution to all infected parts of Tinea's body. It was very painful and he shot out of the MI room. He came back next day looking very glum because the tinea had produced scabs. I put salicylic acid ointment on every tinea ring to soften the scabs. Next day he came back as happy as a king because the scabs had disappeared, rubbed off in the night by the rough sacking he slept in – he'd sold his blanket long before. What remained were clear white rings of skin that hadn't been tanned by the sun. I was amazed. Tinea was exultant and went around the camp showing off his body to blokes returning from their working parties. His transformation set off a small stampede for the 'good stuff' that had made it possible. The MI room's supplies ran out quickly. Ben Adam, the pharmacist, refined the mixture and it became the standard treatment for tinea at the aerodrome camp.

The quiet mornings and afternoons provided an opportunity to learn more about treating ear infections. They were a common problem, often linked to river swimming, and could be very painful with a weeping and crusting eczema-like soreness extending down to the drum. I packed ears with swabs soaked in various drops, and repeated the treatment every two or three days until the problem cleared up. As I became more experienced, I became quite successful at treating a range of ear problems. Even drivers from other camps called in for treatment and I was pleasantly surprised when one or two Japanese guards came.

There weren't many interruptions to the MI room daytime routine. Occasionally I worked with medics from the hospital giving cholera vaccinations. The Japanese provided the vaccine but not new needles. I did hundreds of vaccinations in my time as a prisoner but always faced the same problem: the needles we had were old, blunt from overuse and some were bent. We were stabbing blokes and it hurt like hell. It was particularly bad, and intimidating, when large blunt needles were used for injections in the backside. Blokes squealed, and who could blame them?

One morning a young bloke came in asking for sulphonamide ointment for a troublesome spot on his penis. He didn't want me to see it but I said I couldn't give him anything until I'd examined it. I did and went to Dr de Soldinoff because I suspected syphilis. De Soldinoff confirmed my suspicion and played hell with the bloke because he'd nothing to treat him with except emetine, which was normally used for amoebic dysentery. The officer-soldier relationship transformed quickly into the doctor-patient relationship as de Soldinoff grappled with what he could do. I felt so sorry for the bloke. He'd been to the MI room a few times and shown me photographs of his wife and kids. How was he going to get rid of syphilis? The right drugs weren't available, no one knew whether the next camp on his rotation would prescribe emetine for syphilis, no one knew how long we would remain prisoners, and it was anyone's guess whether his case would be treatable if and when we ever returned to England. This was the only case of syphilis, or venereal disease more generally, that I encountered in three and a half years as a prisoner.

From time to time, a former British medic dropped into the MI room to sit for a while but never to chat. He was mentally ill and shuffled around the camp wearing an Aussie hat and a heavy army cape even on clear sunny days. He never bowed to the guards, who understood the problem: even the hard men were sympathetic. He should have been in hospital but there was no way he'd have stayed. I knew the bloke back in England and at Changi. He came from Bradford and was in the 198th Field Ambulance. He was widely read and had engaged actively with others but clearly had failed to adjust to POW life. Sadly, no one had had the time to look after him because they were busy looking after themselves and their close mates. Engagement had turned into self-imposed isolation, a condition few survived. I met him back in England when we were being demobbed in York in early 1946. He didn't say anything. He was still lost.

The quiet of the late mornings and afternoons ended abruptly with the evening sick parade, which was by far the busiest time of the day. I was fortunate that a mate, often Sammy or Sid, would help when it was very hectic, even though they were tired after working all day in the sun and walking perhaps several miles to and from camp. Much of the evening's work involved malaria cases. Blokes developed malaria during the day while on working parties and came back with soaring temperatures. One fellow's temperature was so high it went off the scale of the thermometer. My job was to take blood samples for analysis by the microbiologist, who had a small laboratory at the hospital. Attending to cuts and injuries always took a great deal of time. On busy nights the MI room wouldn't close much before midnight.

Final months at the aerodrome camp

Patient numbers at the hospital rose slightly through 1944, mainly as a result of malaria and dysentery. The Japanese were keen for men to remain fit and introduced 'glass rodding'. The whole camp went out on parade. Each man lined up in front of several white-coated Japanese officers seated behind an imposing table. We dropped our shorts and underpants, bent over and a Japanese medical officer stuck a glass rod none too gently up our backsides. 'Glass rodding' made you jump and was embarrassing but only happened once or twice and so was tolerable. It may have been part of a general strategy to map the incidence of dysentery across camps and assess prisoners' continuing fitness for hard labour.

The camp hospital had two seriously ill patents during the final months of the year. One had been injured demolishing a hut at the old hospital camp: a heavy cross beam had fallen on his back. Dr de Soldinoff suspected a broken back, though luckily this wasn't the case. A joiner built a wooden convex structure to de Soldinoff's specifications. It was padded, could be straightened over time and could be moved easily. The poor man lay immobile on his back on that structure for months. How he stuck it in all that heat I don't know. All he had to look up at was the attap ceiling of the hospital and the sky when we wheeled him to the slit trenches during air raids. I admired him. He was so cheerful and brave despite being so uncomfortable. I'm glad to say he recovered and learnt to walk again.

The other seriously ill patient had a perforated bowel. Dr de Sold-inoff operated and the man lay on his sleeping platform for around three months, day in, day out, again remaining remarkably cheerful. I often talked to him and from time to time helped to lift him into the trenches during air raids.

The Japanese commandant should be thanked for authorising those slit trenches. Some commandants didn't allow trenches for prisoners and increased Allied bombing through 1944 caused hundreds of casualties. Dozens of prisoners died at Non Pladuk in early September when the rail junction, sidings and workshops were targeted, and there were several deaths at Tamarkan in late November when four bombs fell on the camp. Around 800 prisoners were killed or wounded by Allied bombing in Thailand. This loss could have been reduced if prisoners had received adequate protection.

Air raids up and down the railway increased substantially through 1944. I can't remember any alerts in 1943 at the hospital camp. In fact, I can't remember ever seeing a plane then, but this was to change dramatically. In the first half of 1944, the drone of our heavy bombers started to became familiar as they went to bomb the Bangkok docks and other targets. Japanese or Korean spotters were posted on tall buildings to count incoming planes. There would be some hurried counting of incoming bombers and then the guards would go as fast as they could to safety.

By the second half of the year, there were raids on neighbouring Japanese camps and on the bridge at Tamarkan, but there were no raids on the aerodrome camp. Our planes would dive, drop their bombs and come low over the camp before starting to turn and gain altitude. We waved at them because they were ours and symbolised deliverance and we wanted to make very sure that British and American pilots knew there were POWs in the camp. We all took heart from their bravery and skill, while continuing to worry about being bombed by mistake. The commandant ordered prisoners to stop waving at enemy planes but this was largely ignored. The Japanese sensibly kept their heads well down during these raids and weren't too concerned about what we did.

We were lucky not to be bombed because we were close to Japanese camps, the railway station and the stores depot. A Japanese camp, about 500 yards away, was bombed several times. It was terrifying to see planes dropping objects that looked like sacks of coal, watch them grow larger and larger and then have every sense assaulted by massive explosive forces. I remember the sharp image of a British prisoner, who'd been working at the Japanese camp, illuminated against a background of exploding bombs. He was running desperately along the bamboo perimeter fence of our camp seeking sanctuary within a prison that was a stone's throw away from chaos. 'How do I get in?' he kept shouting, forgetting in his anxiety the whereabouts of the camp's entrance, though he must have passed through it many times.

The railway station and stores also were bombed repeatedly, but our camp was far enough away from them and we avoided casualties.

Towards the end of the year Allied planes flew over our camp most days, going to bomb something or coming back from a raid, and camp security now required the excavation of a substantial ditch, perhaps 20 feet deep and at least 30 feet across, around the entire camp. This was a massive undertaking without mechanical assistance and was similar to the ditch excavated around the camp at Taimuang (Chapter 8). I think similar ditches were carved out around camps across southern Thailand, a reflection of fundamental changes in the world outside the camps: only a few months before a simple bamboo fence, drawbridge and gate had satisfied camp security requirements.

The *Kempeitai*'s presence increased through the year. These stocky little policemen with their fondness for torture, dark glasses and swords that were too big for them, filled everyone with fear. They didn't often make forays into our quarters but were unnecessarily destructive when they did, throwing our kit about with abandon. A lingering look from them made you quake. I remember a lad at the aerodrome camp who was trussed up in a drainage ditch near one of the huts. I managed to talk to him and he said he'd attempted to escape and was waiting for the *Kempeitai*. He thought they were taking him to Singapore for execution.

The *Kempeitai* were horrible little bastards. My most vivid memory of them is being lined up outside a hut as they beat a bloke to death who'd been caught with a radio hidden in a tin of peanuts. We had to stand to attention and listen to his screaming. The beating lasted a long time. I can't say how long but the bastards knew how to prolong this torture and didn't want him to die too quickly. I can still hear those screams. While this was happening, the camp *gunso* sauntered among our ranks, kicking blokes in the shins if they didn't meet his notion of standing to attention. If the purpose of the violence was to provide an object lesson in why not to build and operate a radio, it was very effective.

We speculated endlessly on the meaning of all this bombing, digging and secret police activity. We also speculated on what the Japanese were trying to achieve by making propaganda films at this time about our 'privileged' lives as prisoners. We were filmed resplendent in new clothes we'd never see again, within drooling distance of fine foods we'd never eat and holding tennis rackets we'd never use to hit a ball. Did the air strikes mean the end of the war was just around the corner? Did all the digging anticipate possible landings by paratroops and attempts to arm prisoners? Was the stage being set for a defensive tussle that might outlive us? Was the filming part of a strategy to rewrite history in preparation for a post-war world when we'd be reconciled?

Chapter 8

Starving in Central Thailand: The Last Six Months

By January 1945, I'd spent two years in the Kanchanaburi area. I was stale and kept remembering a hot and very dry day some months earlier when a bush fire had threatened a Japanese lookout post high up in the hills. A group of us were taken by truck to fight the fire. It was a fool's errand because we weren't given any fire fighting equipment but it was so good being in the hills and looking out on line after line of jagged ranges to the west. Only one bored guard supervised us – it was enough because plunging into that dry bush without food, water, maps, compass, and a support system would have been deadly – but that day gave me the illusion of freedom. I didn't want to stay couped up in Kanchanaburi any longer.

I was pleased when the order came in mid-January to leave the aerodrome camp as part of the regular cycle of change within the camps. As we boarded the barges to take us downstream, I hoped we might see something of the country and not be confined to another camp, but none of us were surprised when we were towed 8 to 9 miles downstream to the camp at Taimuang. It was a logical rotation because of its large hospital. What was surprising was being uprooted from the hospital after a couple of months, put on boats and towed to Bangkok, and then packed into steel-sided railway trucks – identical to the ones we'd travelled in to southern Thailand two years earlier – and taken to central Thailand.

Taimuang and Bangkok

I arrived at Taimuang with a group of medics. The vast camp was surrounded by a ditch worthy of an Iron Age hill fort and made in the same backbreaking way. Various parts of the camp were sub-divided by their own ditches. The hospital had its own huge

97

grounds – walking around them was more than enough exercise. It served several hundred patients, predominantly dysentery and malaria cases.

There was nothing unusual about this. What was unusual was the level of security. Security at the aerodrome camp had been tightened over the previous year as attacks on the railway increased and the war turned decisively against Japan in Burma and the Pacific. But the level of security at Taimuang was of a different order of magnitude. It was as if they feared imminent landings by our paratroops. The *Kempeitai* were a louring presence and Japanese soldiers made hourly checks through the night on POW numbers in every hospital ward and in the huts occupied by fit blokes assigned to the various working parties.

In the hospital, night duty orderlies managed this constant checking; in the working huts, blokes were rostered through the night. Reconciling actual and required numbers was worked out with the guard in Japanese. This took some doing because the numbers became long and complex but this wasn't the hard part. The hard part, particularly in dysentery wards, was accounting for men visiting the latrine. At one level this was simple. Patients using the latrine were instructed to move bamboo sticks from a small container kept in the ward to a large one and then reverse this when they returned to the ward. Three sticks, for example, in the large container meant there were three men in the latrine; this number would then be added to the number of men physically identified on their sleeping platforms, and the total (hopefully) would add up to the full complement. At an operational level, reconciling numbers was far from simple. For the tally to be out only required one patient to be careless or to forget to move the bamboo sticks correctly in his haste to reach the latrine. Frustrated guards might then lash out and an exercise that should take ten minutes every hour, and be manageable with juggling other night shift duties, would drag on interminably. It would end only when the numbers tallied.

In the short time I was at Taimuang, the *Kempeitai* used an attap hut outside the camp. It was entirely bare with a dirt floor and no sleeping platforms. I saw the inside only once. The *Kempeitai* were looking for a spy with links to the Thai resistance. They suspected one of our patients, perhaps on the slender basis that he had a Malay wife in Singapore. Sammy and I were ordered to bring the patient – a sailor – to the hut for interrogation. There were several prisoners kneeling, heads bowed and spaced around the hut so they couldn't communicate with one another. *Kempeitai* officers walked casually around the room, split canes in hand, occasionally lashing the kneeling men who didn't make a sound. We were ordered to put the stretcher down, leave the patient on the floor and wait outside, for which we were thankful. We expected to hear screaming but fortunately didn't.

Our patient convinced the *Kempeitai* that he wasn't their man. Perhaps he'd done nothing or was just very fortunate. After an hour or so, we were told to take the man back to camp. Carrying a patient on a stretcher for any distance isn't easy. Normally we would rest every so often but on that day we ran all the way to the camp drawbridge, fearing the sods might change their minds. We only stopped running once we entered the illusory security of our camp. We were tired out and the sailor was relieved, even after the bumpy ride back. There was nothing much to say. If he'd been a spy or involved in some clandestine activity, he wouldn't have discussed it with us: if he were innocent, he needed time to repair his shattered nerves.

In mid-March 1945, the Japanese moved at least one group of about 300 prisoners out of Taimuang. There were some medics among them but most were infantry and all were judged to be fit by prevailing standards. The transfer was done with the usual secrecy and without prior warning. I was happy to be on the move again when I knew that the group included Bill Graham and some of my mates from the cigarette racket. Captain Marks, who had transferred from the aerodrome camp to Taimuang at the same time as us, was appointed as one of the two medical officers. The other was an Australian surgeon – Captain Beresford. We assembled at the camp jetty, embarked on barges and were towed downriver.

We arrived at the Bangkok docks at night and were billeted in a damaged warehouse. Its concrete floor was broken and mostly covered with mounds of sand. Sleeping on it was comfortable and we had a good night's rest. Next morning, British prisoners, who were working as stevedores and were billeted next door, told us the sand covered an unexploded bomb. We were so inured to the threat of death by this time that we weren't overly concerned. Anyway, the Japanese wouldn't have allowed us to move out of the warehouse even if we had been. We just hoped the damn thing wouldn't go off while we were around. The blokes next door must have felt the same because an explosion would have blown them to kingdom come too. The mounds of sand wouldn't have made much difference.

More importantly, we were told that the docks were being heavily bombed and, at the first sign of a raid, we must cross the railway sidings and get away from the dock area. They emphasised that the Japanese never stopped anyone from running away because they were too busy getting out of harm's way themselves. This was good advice. We were in Bangkok for two days waiting for a train and were bombed on each of them. We suffered one serious casualty. An Aussie took refuge among a pile of steel girders during an air raid. A bomb landed close by and a girder was blasted into the air and came down cleanly cutting off one of his legs, leaving no skin flaps to place over the open wound. He was brave, stoic despite his great pain, and his stump had the disturbing habit of shaking when we dressed it.

Leaving Bangkok was a relief. We travelled slowly east for a couple of days, stopping occasionally for food and water, toilet breaks and supplies for the locomotive. The region seemed to be untouched by the war. When the train finally stopped, we were ordered to get off in something like a paddy field. There was no railway station and there were no local people. No one told us where we were and we didn't have maps. From the train we had a full day's march to what was intended to become a transit camp. An advanced party had erected one hut. Our initial task was to complete the camp.

Region around Nakhon Nayok: mid-March to early May
I faced my new life with a ragged shirt, a pair of shorts that were slowly rotting, a loincloth that I wore most of the time to preserve my shorts, a pair of rubber sandals with canvass tops, a pair of clip-clops – wooden-soled sandals with a strap over the big toe – a pair of socks, a mosquito net, my medical bag, a couple of water bottles, a mess tin, and a razor with blunt blades. The other blokes were in much the same boat. Some had groundsheets. A tiny few had managed to maintain their boots and some had boots that were only partly rotted and serviceable to some degree. The officers had enough clothing to look tidy, but most wandered around in shorts, no shirt and clip-clops. You could walk for miles in them once you got used to them.

100

We were put to work building huts and digging latrines. The handful of Japanese guards – we never saw any Koreans in central and eastern Thailand – wanted us to construct four substantial huts, with a hospital occupying half of one of them, and a small mortuary. They also wanted a latrine dug of monumental proportions: it was to be about 20 feet deep with no side supports because of the rock-like nature of the ground. Digging the latrine was hot, exhausting work, but the pace slackened once it was completed and we'd built basic accommodation for the working party. The guards didn't seem to mind this. There was no hectoring or beatings. They told us what they wanted, kept an eye on the construction and kept mostly to themselves. We too kept to ourselves and were not disturbed after evening rollcall. The war, and the terror of Taimuang, seemed a long way away as we settled down after our evening meal to play bridge and chess. We didn't know it at the time but this would be the last time we'd be playing games.

Our general health at this early stage was reasonable. The Aussie who'd lost his leg in Bangkok needed careful treatment, there were a few blokes with mild dysentery and there were the inevitable cases of malaria. In the month spent building the transit camp, one bloke died of malaria. I prepared him for burial late one evening but didn't do a good job. I wrapped him in sacks but didn't plug effectively all outlets and tie up the chin to prevent the mouth from dropping open. Next day I was shocked to find froth on the sacking nearest his mouth. Air escaping from his body had produced it but it shook me. For a few moments I thought I'd trussed up an unconscious man and left him to die.

Once the transit camp was built, our working party was subdivided and sent on different routes to work on jungle roads. My sub-group had about 100 men in it, including Dr Marks as medical officer and my mate Sid Browne. Another sub-group included Bill Graham, Sammy Robinson and Iggy.

The first twenty-five members of our group and the whole group's rice supply left in two trucks escorted by a couple of Japanese guards. The rest of the blokes were to follow when transport became available. The trip got off to a bad start. The trucks lumbered along jungle roads that were bad during the day and treacherous at night. The drivers were running behind schedule and pressed on after dark. Oddly, the lead driver didn't use his headlights or maybe didn't have any. What light there was came from the headlights of the following truck. An accident was predictable: running into a steamroller 'parked' across the track was not. The truck wouldn't move again without major repairs. The blokes in it were shaken but the sacks of rice had cushioned their falls. Only one fellow was badly injured. Dr Marks suspected a fractured pelvis.

The one good thing about the accident was that it occurred near a Japanese camp that had a hospital. The remaining truck took Dr Marks and the injured bloke there. Marks explained the problem to Japanese doctors who agreed to examine the patient. Fortunately, the man was just hurt and worse for wear and his pelvis wasn't fractured. He celebrated by passing water. He'd been holding on for hours because, apparently, you shouldn't pass water in the normal way with a fractured pelvis. Dr Marks didn't have the tubes and other equipment required for a temporary bypass and, even if he had, performing an operation on a jungle road at night in poor light wouldn't have been a good idea.

After two or three days, our whole party of 100 men arrived by one means or another at a jungle camp and was met by Japanese road engineers, who took over the guarding role and set us to work. They were an unusual group. They were taller than the average Japanese and some seemed fat, perhaps because I was so thin. They were well dressed and seemed well educated. They were pleasant at times, even friendly, allowing blokes suffering from malaria to ride on the rice truck that accompanied us for part of the march. At other times, especially if they felt under pressure to meet targets, they could be rotten sods, but even then they never went out of their way to be harsh. I think their hearts and souls just weren't into repairing jungle roads. They were as fed up as we were.

The engineers led us on a route march along jungle tracks. One engineer, who was marching near me, was carrying a heavy machine-gun and was drenched in sweat. The trek was taking its toll on him. He was not happy and I was determined to give no offence. This first long trek also was taking its toll on the rest of us. We had nothing to eat all day. Some blokes came down with malaria and friends were carrying them. We didn't know where we were going or how long we'd be marching. After nightfall it was difficult just staying on the track and we clung to the bloke in front of us. We must have resembled a gigantic 'crocodile' of primary school children or a chain gang.

It was pitch black when we were ordered to halt. We dropped our kit, spread out groundsheets and flopped down for the night. After a few minutes I felt something crawl over my face before disappearing in the undergrowth. I thought it was a snake but it was too dark to see and I was too frightened to be certain. I shouted 'snake' as loudly as I could and we collectively discovered reserves of energy to start making fires. A few fires were lit and there was enough light to reveal a clearing that must have been used as a staging point by previous working parties. It was like a gigantic latrine.

Next day we continued the march to a point where the engineers told working parties to fan out to repair dirt roads to make them suitable for trucks. Many roads were in a bad state of repair. Work mostly involved cutting down trees and positioning them over washed-out sections of road. Blokes were out from early morning until dusk and worked seven days a week. It was hard labour but our general health was sound at this stage, and thoughts of the variegated splendour of the jungle could still intrude on the more practical business of coping with exhaustion. Blokes came down with malaria of course, and mates carried them or, if the road engineers brought the truck, rode on the rice sacks at the back of it. The engineers were not slave drivers, perhaps realising as well as we did that a good job required more than blunt axes, *chunkals* (an Asian digging implement that is like a cross between a spade and a hoe) and minimum rations – we were hungry all of the time in central Thailand. Progress on road repairs was slow and superficial. The norm was for working parties to march to a section of road identified by the engineers, spend a day or two repairing the worst damage and move on.

After a couple of weeks, we were ordered to march again. The march started badly with an argument between a British sergeant and the Japanese *gunso* over a British refusal to share tea with the Japanese. It was a stupid stunt to pull because the two sergeants had been getting on well together. The *gunso* kicked over all the buckets of boiling water on our fires so no one had anything to drink. He then ordered a fast march. This was hard on everyone. We were all exhausted and desperate for a drink by mid-afternoon when the *gunso* finally ordered a halt. The British sergeant offered to make tea for the Japanese. The offer was accepted, a fire was lit, water was boiled, and we hoped fervently that some tea would be left for us.

103

It didn't work out like that either for the Japanese or us. The British prisoner preparing the tea was a scruffy fellow who always wore a filthy sweat rag around his neck. He removed the rag to lift the tea can from the fire and the rag fell into the tea. The Japanese saw this as another insult and went wild. The *gunso* kicked over the tea can and ordered another fast march. When we stopped for the night he wouldn't let us light fires so we faced the prospect of going without a meal and not being able to drink anything because we couldn't risk drinking unboiled water.

To cap off a thoroughly bad day, the *gunso* resumed his argument with the British sergeant, in the process picking up a pumpkin from the rice truck to hurl at him. The pumpkin was rotten and slimy. It went up in the air and landed on the head of a Japanese guard. The rotten pumpkin trickled down his face but he never moved a muscle in front of the *gunso*. It was a comedy show without laughter, though the *gunso* showed a flicker of a smile. After a few minutes he calmed down and gave us permission to light fires so we could make tea and have some hot food. No king dining on the finest foods could ever have derived more satisfaction from a meal than we did that night dining on rice and vegetable stew washed down with mugs of unsweetened black tea.

The march continued next day. The British sergeant came down with malaria. There was no point asking the *gunso* if he could ride on the rice truck so blokes took it in turns to carry him for the best part of 10 miles. On this march, a small hole in my sock created a blister on my right heel. The blister grew under the hard skin, which peeled off exposing raw flesh. I couldn't walk normally but had miles more to walk that day and, unbeknown to me, faced the prospect of walking several hundred miles on one foot and the toes of the other in coming months: eventually I couldn't straighten my right leg.

Having decent footwear on long marches is so important and hardly any of us had it. One bloke had no footwear at all. I don't know how he walked all those miles over rough ground. He must have gone through agony until his feet toughened up. My sandals soon disintegrated. The rubber soles and remnants of canvas uppers were held together by pieces of string and jungle creepers. Without boots, blokes' feet were cut so easily and cuts frequently turned septic. I came to hate night marches because you never knew

104

where you were putting your feet. My constant fear was losing a rubber sole in a bog. Fortunately, it happened only once, and I found it.

There was no pretence of working on the roads and no going around in circles. We marched to Nakhon Nayok, a town in eastern Thailand that was in the middle of new Japanese defensive positions. For years I believed we'd marched to Phnom Penh – someone must have mentioned it and the name stuck because it was one of the few in the region I was familiar with from school geography.

If the quays, administrative offices, Buddhist temples, parks, markets, and paved streets were a good deal smaller than those in the real Phnom Penh, Nakhon Nayok was a wonderful 'other world'. People were well dressed, promenaded the pavements and read newspapers in cafés. A few stared at us as we marched through their town. We were jungle men, filthy, sweaty and unshaven. We wore rags. At least half of us just wore loincloths. Some blokes tried to speak to the locals but there was no response, presumably because of the strong Japanese presence and not wanting to invite trouble. Sensing the gulf between us, we started to sing songs like *Land of Hope and Glory*, *Rule Britannia* and *There'll Always be an England*. No one tried to stop us, but the incongruity between our stirring words and our servitude must have struck many as eccentric or even delusional.

We were billeted in the grounds of an old temple and did no work in the town in the few days we were there. The Japanese guards didn't pester us. There were the usual roll-calls but nothing excessive. We were free to swim in the fast flowing river and clean ourselves up. A few blokes attempted to talk to the local women doing their washing there, but understandably they were given no encouragement. We tended the sick – the number of blokes with malaria kept on rising – and buried one bloke who died from blackwater fever, a terrible form of malaria.

March to Phitsanulok

The march began again on 8 May. Our undeclared destination was Phitsanulok in north central Thailand, a march of 375 miles, our purpose to establish a work camp there and upgrade the network of jungle roads. We were the advanced party of supposedly fit men and Dr Marks once again was our medical officer. I was pleased about this: we got on well together and I think a friendship emerged

105

within the strictures of the doctor-orderly relationship. A larger party followed in early June. After the war I found out that Dr Poh was the medical officer for that group. I knew him at the Kanchanaburi Hospital Camp in 1943 but sadly we never met again.

For a couple of weeks or so it was the same routine as in March and April: our working party marched to points identified by the road engineers and then groups moved out cutting down trees and repairing roads as best they could. The difference was that both the blokes and the engineers didn't seem to care at all about the tasks at hand. The engineers lost their truck but acquired an old, heavy wooden cart to carry their rice supplies, tents and cooking gear. Unfortunately, they didn't acquire a bullock to pull it: this was done by teams of prisoners.

Perhaps in response to orders to work harder and faster, the engineers split the working party into two teams, which were put to work on different sections of road. The idea was to cut down on the time spent walking to jobs and allow teams to operate further along the jungle tracks. Our group was led by Regimental Sergeant Major Bennett – and I became the group's de facto medical officer. Dr Marks was the medical officer of the other group and my mate Sid Browne was ordered to accompany him.

Engineers with targets to meet now pushed harder for full work teams and were increasingly intolerant of illness-related excuses. For the first time, I experienced this pressure directly. I felt desperately alone: I was separated from my mates, the Japanese were putting pressure on me and I had no one to go to for medical advice. The engineers bullied but never overturned my decisions on who could and couldn't work, which they might easily have done because I didn't have a doctor's authority. This brief experience demonstrated to me just how difficult it must have been for doctors earlier in our captivity to declare blokes unfit for work – and stick to those decisions – in the face of sustained and intense pressure to turn out full work quotas.

The engineers decided they could boost productivity further by splitting off a group of about fifteen men and establishing an out-lying work camp some 7 or 8 miles further up the jungle road. The initiative didn't last for more than a few days, but the engineers gave me permission to visit the group on condition that I took their weekly rice rations. I set off pushing a wheelbarrow containing a sack of rice and carrying a shoulder bag with my medical supplies.

106

By this stage the bag was very light, with just a few bandages, gauze and some sulphonamide paste. I didn't even have quinine. I learnt later that Dr Marks' supplies were almost as depleted, but it must have been more frustrating for him because he was expected to perform miracles without medicines. This was precisely what doctors had been doing for the past three years, and were required to continue doing.

Going to the work camp by myself felt very strange. I was entirely alone for the first time in years and I didn't like it. It was so quiet in the damp warmth and green light and the hairs on the back of my neck stood up as I imagined being watched by unfriendly eyes. It was nonsense, of course. There were no hungry animals prowling around during the day or savage tribesmen lurking behind the bushes, but I was much relieved when I arrived at the work camp. I examined all the blokes. They appeared to have no pressing medical problems and I thought myself fortunate to return to the main camp just before nightfall. A night spent alone on a jungle track would have been hard on the nerves.

That sense of good fortune lasted about a couple of days. A bloke became very sick with what appeared to be appendicitis. Dr Marks and his work team were many miles away and couldn't be reached, but there were Japanese camps in the immediate area. A Japanese doctor was visiting them and the engineers facilitated a meeting with him at our camp. He confirmed my diagnosis, adding in reasonable English that the man would probably die within twenty-four hours without an operation. He told me he couldn't perform the appendicectomy because of urgent commitments at Japanese camps and I would have to do it, even though I wasn't a doctor. I asked him for equipment, hoping this might change his mind. It didn't. He supplied a scalpel, forceps, gauze, swabs, and some chloroform before hurrying off.

I'd watched Dr de Soldinoff perform appendicectomies at the Kanchanaburi Hospital Camp in 1943, but there is a world of difference between observing and doing. I was terrified and the prospect of operating in the jungle miles from any assistance filled me with horror. I knew virtually nothing and the little I knew decreased in proportion to my rising anxiety. I didn't even know how long the effects of chloroform would last, never mind how to cut open a living man. I prayed harder than I've ever prayed in my life. It didn't matter that God and religion weren't part of my life any more. At that moment they were central to my being. I mopped the bloke's brow to cool him down a little. I had to do something. Thankfully, the man's condition eased gradually and he started to improve and the pain subsided. I can't claim this transformation had anything to do with me or with prayer or with luck, but I was massively relieved and thankful, whatever the reason.

After two or three weeks, the two work teams were reunited again and by then the engineers had lost whatever residual enthusiasm they had for repairing jungle roads. Conditions were very bad. Food, safe water and medicines were scarce. The mosquitoes were relentless and we'd run out of quinine. The rain was coming down in torrents every day, drenching everyone and everything. We were always wet.

About this time, supervision of the working party was taken over by front line infantry who'd just returned from Burma. We were apprehensive. They were tiny chaps with little black beards and looked rough and tough, which was understandable given the battlegrounds they'd just come from. We marched together every day for several weeks avoiding villages and small towns, or at least not seeing them. There were no working parties fixing roads or anything else. It all seemed to be without purpose but was fairly civilised. These little fellows were the very best guards I ever encountered in my years as a POW. They were not in the least aggressive. Unlike the engineers, they didn't have a truck or cart to carry their rice supplies, tents and other equipment. They didn't have much – Japanese supply lines to Burma weren't working effectively by 1945 – but what they had they carried themselves. There was no expectation that we would carry it for them.

The food situation was grim both for the Japanese and us. Some blokes with a modicum of botanical knowledge offered suggestions on what might be eaten safely. One of the highlights was finding something like wild spinach. We saw plenty of spiders and ants but not too many snakes or birds, which was a pity because we'd have killed and eaten them. We were down to mugs of tea, half a cup of watery rice porridge for breakfast, half a cup of cooked rice sprinkled with rock salt for lunch and full cups of cooked rice and vegetable-flavoured water for dinner. This tested everyone's capacity to manage food rationing. From the beginning of the march, each bloke was responsible for carrying his personal weekly rice supply. If this wasn't done effectively, he went short towards the end of the week and no one, not even close mates, could afford to share with him.

In these conditions sickness increased among prisoners and guards alike. The Japanese officer in command of the infantry unit had a bad case of tinea, which he asked me to treat. During one of the treatments he apologised for the lack of food, saying he didn't want prisoners to suffer and had requested more food from his senior officer, but the request had been denied. Some of the Japanese had bad leg ulcers, which we cleaned and treated with sulphonamide paste. The Japanese were considerate towards our sick, some even sharing their own meagre food rations with them. Malaria was our big problem and there were a few cases of dysentery. We didn't have stretchers, which meant mates had to carry those who couldn't walk. Having good mates now was crucial for survival.

The infantrymen were wonderful fellows and we were genuinely sorry when they had to leave for other duties. There were handshakes all round and kind words. These fellows didn't have anything to prove to men who couldn't defend themselves, which was part of the problem with some of the Korean guards in Thailand. They were good soldiers and decent people.

The road engineers took over again. We continued to march upwards of 10 miles each day without knowing, or really caring, about where we were going. For some reason that I've never been able to understand, we didn't use the train that could have taken us further north and saved weeks of marching. We weren't even pretending to repair jungle roads any more and our general health was in steep decline. The majority of blokes had ulcers on their legs and feet. Ulcer cases started to appear early in the march, and there was a plethora of cases after we waded through apparently clear water that turned out to be full of leeches. Leeches have to be burnt off and ulcers often form where they bite into the skin. I was lucky not to have ulcers on my legs and feet but had one at the base of my left thumb, the result of a small cut that was infected by dirty dressings. I bathed the ulcer repeatedly and dressed it with sulphonamide paste but it made little difference. The flesh continued to be eaten away.

The ulcers were nowhere near as bad as the ones we'd seen in mid-1943 when human wrecks started to come down from upcountry work camps by train and barge, but they were bad enough and became worse over time. The Japanese didn't give us any medicines – their supplies were low. Even soap and disinfectant to wash bandages would have been useful, but we didn't get that either.

At the end of each day's march, the medical work began. Dr Marks held a sick parade and did whatever he could to keep blokes going. Sid Browne and I spent at least a couple of hours boiling water, taking off gauze dressings, cleaning ulcers, boiling recycled bandages and drying them for use the next day. It took about ten to fifteen minutes to deal with each man, so different groups were dealt with each night. I don't think Sid and I did a better job than most blokes did by themselves, but it always seemed better if someone else did the cleaning and washing, though the pain may have been the same. Scraping off rotten flesh without chloroform was the worst part and was terribly painful.

The proliferation of ulcers was a hard blow coming on top of malaria, which was now out of control. Dysentery had once again emerged as a significant problem. Around this time it claimed the life of one bloke. The poor chap knew we could do nothing for him and he was dying, and day after day he was jolted up and down in the back of a wooden cart. What an uncomfortable death it must have been. We couldn't bury him properly because the ground was too rocky, so we dug a shallow grave, laid the man in it, covered the grave with stones to keep out foraging animals, and erected a crude cross. There was no way to identify the location to the War Graves Commission: it was a lonely spot to bury a British serviceman.

Slow starvation, lack of medicines and lack of hope led to a rapid deterioration in health levels as the march dragged on. Food had always been an obsession for us in Changi and Kanchanaburi but this was something quite different. It was a gnawing emptiness that filled every moment and made you desperate to look for anything that might be edible, which would then be scrutinised meticulously. We became shadows of the men we'd been. But oddly there was no significant increase in avitaminosis diseases. Perhaps blokes had become accustomed to a low vitamin diet after so many years of being POWs or there was significant nutritional value in some of the plants we were taking from the jungle or there were entirely different factors at work.

We didn't come across villages and towns until the end of the war so the option of trading for food didn't exist. Besides, we had virtually nothing of value to trade. All our clothes were rags. Morale

110

was at rock bottom. By August 1945 I hadn't the slightest inkling the war was almost over and was convinced I'd never be free. Some of my mates in the working party were resigned to the same fate. We were so very isolated. For all we knew, the march and the war would drag on forever.

I felt abandoned. Who could ever find us if a rescue were to be mounted? Who would know if we simply disappeared? I tried not to dwell on these sorts of things because they were unresolvable and poisoned morale. The road engineers weren't cruel men but they were ill-tempered and disillusioned, and they were the ones carrying machine-guns. There was safety in numbers in the big camps. On remote jungle roads we were aware of our vulnerability, though in fairness to the engineers there wasn't even the faintest sense that we were on a death march and faced possible massacre. We had more pressing things to think about: we were stuck in a day-to-day battle for survival.

At this low point, two things lifted my spirits. The first was meeting up unexpectedly in early August with Bill Graham, Sammy, Iggy and other friends from their working party. Like us, they had been on their own march to nowhere, repairing roads in some places but mostly marching aimlessly around the country-side. We now numbered around 200, which felt reassuring. It was wonderful having Bill back as leader and organiser and having more close mates to look out for one another.

The other good thing was that a British Infantryman met members of the Thai resistance by chance, joined them and the road engineers didn't take any action to recapture him. We expected at least the standard punishment of standing on parade for hours in the sun and came prepared for it with water bottles, cooked rice in our mess tins, shirts and hats – a few blokes still had hats – but the engineers didn't seem overly concerned. They'd lost interest in the war. One POW more or less didn't seem to matter any more. Unlike all the useless rumours that circulated, that was the first piece of hard evidence that the world might be changing.

August–September – freedom delayed
In mid-August, we stopped at a small village and some blokes asked for permission to buy tobacco with the few cents they'd been hoarding. They came back very excited because the Thais had told them the war was over, Japan had surrendered and all Allied

prisoners were free. Someone had even produced a child's slate and chalk to spell it out in English. We were excited but sceptical.

Sergeant Major Bennett told us to calm down and expect nothing. He was a perceptive man and must have been worried about how the Japanese would react when they realised they'd lost the war. He told us to show no signs of high spirits that we might be free and definitely not debate with the Japanese about freedom because they had the guns and we didn't know their orders or how they might carry them out. We weren't a rabble – discipline existed – and we listened carefully to these wise words and kept our emotions in check. But we couldn't sleep that night, especially after seeing a plane fly over with its navigation lights on – something we hadn't seen before. We felt the war had to be over and yearned for confirmation next day on the march.

The march got off to an excellent start and soared to new heights by mid-morning when we met a group of Thais bowling along the jungle road in what we called a 'piggy' bus – a bus for people and anything else that could be crammed into it. These people were so different from the Thais we'd known in the past. The difference was that the war was over. They could say what they wanted. They were no longer afraid of the Japanese and didn't want them in their country. They leant out of the windows shouting and cheering, exulting at our freedom and theirs, and asking the question by signs, gestures and tones: why were we still marching as prisoners under the Japanese?

The answer, of course, was that the Japanese had machine-guns. We couldn't do anything against them and so kept on marching. Before nightfall we came to a village and were billeted at a school. Sergeant Major Bennett met the Japanese officer commanding the engineering unit and asked whether the war was over. The officer said he had received no orders to that effect, we were still his prisoners and we would be shot if we didn't obey orders. Bennett came back and said something like: 'Chaps, we may be free but don't start any funny business because he says you'll be shot. He means it. It's not worth it at this stage. Take it steady. We're so close to going home.'

We had to accept this outcome and next morning set out on a full day's march that took us to a small township. When we arrived 100 or so people lined up on a wooden bridge on the town's outskirts, happily cheering us and saying we were free. The Japanese didn't like it but didn't interfere. During the night, a handful of blokes sneaked out of our billet. They found two Japanese guards on the wooden bridge. In a rush of madness, they overpowered them, took their watches and rings – just as the Japanese had done to us after the fall of Singapore – and flung the guards into a river swollen with monsoon rain. I dread to think what would have happened to us if the guards had managed to drag themselves out of the river and raise the alarm. It was the sort of incident that could have sparked a slaughter. The Japanese never raised the guards' disappearance with us and we never raised it with our own authorities or anyone else.

The march continued next day. It must have been towards the end of August. The engineers led us to a Japanese garrison town. I think it may have been Phitsanulok or somewhere nearby. Soldiers were in good uniforms and their officers were immaculate. But the town itself looked odd. There were numerous wooden terrace houses and Japanese everywhere were poking their heads out of windows and grinning at us. One stupid bloke started shouting at them and acted out lopping off heads. Grins turned sombre.

We stayed for a week or so to the beginning of September. Huts were assigned; we were barb-wired in (though in a largely tokenistic way) and had roll-calls each evening. The Japanese obviously knew about the surrender and our being free but this was never communicated to us formally. On our first night there, the prisoners as a body – except for the medics, who stayed with the sick – refused to remain confined, broke down part of the flimsy fence and started to walk into the town. They were stopped by machine-gun fire. It was not directed at them but was close enough to show that the Japanese meant business. The blokes ran back behind the fence but six were caught and tied up outside the guardroom. They were trussed up in the usual unpleasant way: a wire or rope went around their necks, passed down their backs and wrapped around their wrists, which were pinned behind their backs. This ensured they'd choke if their bodies sagged or their heads went forward, so it forced them to sit almost bolt upright. Inevitably, necks were bruised and hurt.

Next day, Sergeant Major Bennett again met the Japanese officer commanding the engineering unit, who presumably had been fully briefed on Japan's surrender, and demanded the immediate release of the six men from the guardroom, the same quality of food as the Japanese received, and the termination of Japanese authority over

113

his men. The six blokes were released immediately, we were given quinine and other medicines, and our diets improved – we were given chickens – but there was no concession on being allowed out of camp. The barbed wire stayed. We were free to all intents and purposes but were not jumping for joy because we remained under Japanese control. It was explained that the Imperial Japanese Army was responsible for our welfare and we must remain under its authority, as it would be accountable for any 'mishaps' to prisoners under a framework 'negotiated' with the British Commander-in-Chief, Lord Mountbatten. With the exception of dispensing immediately with daily or twice daily roll-calls, this position never changed in the next few days.

What did change was an isolated outbreak of smallpox. Within a day or so of coming to the garrison town, one bloke came down with the disease. He had blisters all over his body and was a ghastly sight. He just lay inertly on his blanket on the sleeping platform and hardly made a sound. He must have been in agony but there was next to nothing we could do for him. We couldn't bathe him – he was a horror of blisters – and well-tried palliatives like moistening the mouth with glycerine provided no benefit. He was semiconscious for almost all of the time and was dead well within a week, so his suffering wasn't too protracted.

We burnt the body. Like at Kanchanaburi Hospital Camp when we burnt the body of a cholera victim, the Japanese facilitated matters but didn't involve themselves directly. They limited their involvement to authorising some Thais to bring in wood for the funeral pyre and giving us permission to burn the body within our barbed wired enclosure.

How the man contracted smallpox was never discovered but clearly he had never been vaccinated. About thirty blokes, including some medics, developed a mild form of the disease that amounted to a few spots on the body and a general feeling of being unwell. All had been vaccinated, so the disease didn't take hold or spread in a lethal way.

The medical team dealing with the outbreak included Sammy, Iggy, Sid Browne, and me, led by Dr Marks. I worried because I'd not been vaccinated against smallpox. Doctors back in England had tried to vaccinate me three times but it hadn't taken and I was told I had natural immunity. I hoped the doctors were right. I was confident but reality is a harsh test.

114

Every infected person was isolated at one end of a long hut where some of us slept. There was no physical barrier marking the isolation area; rather it was an imaginary line beyond which the smallpox contact cases could not go. The Japanese provided vaccine so everyone – contacts and the rest – could be re-vaccinated for additional protection. Sid and I did around 100 vaccinations each, working at the opposite end of the long hut from the isolation area. The fact that we came from the isolation area ourselves, and therefore risked spreading the disease, was hardly best practice, but there was no one else outside the isolation area to do the work and the Japanese doctors wouldn't do it. Their objectives were to provide the vaccine and ensure we didn't go beyond the barbed wire strung around our huts. Similarly, we broke quarantine to clean and dress ulcers and work with malaria and dysentery patients. All this was done within a few yards of the isolation area. The disregard for strict quarantine was of no concern either to the contact cases or the rest of the men. They had been vaccinated in the past and had now been re-vaccinated; there was no real prospect of the mild cases suddenly turning worse; and morale was very high because we were eating better food, the war was over and we were going home.

At the start of September, the Japanese told us to prepare to leave the town. A convoy of trucks and their Thai drivers arrived one night and took us to the railway station. No Japanese appeared to watch our departure (and I didn't see another Japanese soldier or civilian during the rest of my time in Southeast Asia), but they must have organised our transport to the south of Thailand. They hadn't relinquished their authority over the country and no other organisation existed at this time that could have managed the transport and logistics.

We went in open cattle trucks. Medics and the smallpox contact cases went in one truck, which had a red blanket tied securely on one side to signal danger. At roughly the halfway point we stopped at a station where good quality fried rice and jugs of boiled water were set out for us. The isolation cases were allowed out of the wagon when everyone else had eaten. Food and water containers were set on the ground, the 'able bodied' retreated to safety and we moved forward to start eating and drinking. It was like a scene from a medieval mystery play. This feeding drama was staged once more as we travelled further south. The train finally stopped at a nondescript camp in southern Thailand, close to a jungle runway that was big enough for Dakotas to take off and land. I never knew its name. I've always called it the Dakota Camp.

Conclusions

Nineteen-forty-five combined the best and the worst of times for me as a POW. Hearing belatedly and unexpectedly that Japan had surrendered, and knowing it was true, was the single most exquisite moment of happiness in my life. It was an amazing moment of pure joy when I literally felt a warming of my inner being and when all things seemed possible. The feeling didn't last long. Joy quickly became tinged with sadness as memories surfaced of all the friends and all the others who had longed for this day and hadn't made it. That feeling lasted much longer. And, over time, feelings of joy were tested by impatience. Like everyone else, I wanted to go home as quickly as possible but sat around waiting for something to happen. It was frustrating.

Central Thailand is mostly memorable as the worst period in my life as a POW. I was hobbling on one foot and the toes of the other for hundreds of miles and was haunted by the fear of falling by the wayside. We were starving to death. We were overwhelmed by disease. We were closed off from the rest of the world. We were vulnerable to the road engineers turning on us, however unlikely. And, arguably, we were moving towards the conditions that prevailed in up-country work camps in the summer of 1943, though this was still some way off. The work pressures were much less and there wasn't the brutality.

We also were engaged in something that was utterly pointless. For a short while we debated the purpose of the intermittent road-work but there were far better things to talk about. Thinking about it now, the Japanese wanted to upgrade the jungle roads to reinforce their defensive positions in eastern Thailand or facilitate a co-ordinated retreat into Indo-China if the Allies couldn't be held, or prepare in some way for a last stand. If there was a grand purpose behind what we were doing, we and the other working parties did nothing to advance it. The effectiveness of the jungle road network barely changed.

FREEDOM

Chapter 9

The Joy and Fear of Freedom

At last, at the Dakota Camp, I was free. It was early September 1945. I was in a hut with smallpox cases surrounded by barbed wire, but I was no longer a prisoner of war. I was happy and relieved; the oppression of the last three and a half years had evaporated. In less than two month's time I would be back in England.

Those two months were a period of never-ending waiting, staying close to mates who'd held together through the ups and downs of captivity, catching up with old friends from Changi and Kanchanaburi, catching up with what had happened in the world, and trying to imagine the new post-war world and my place in it. Most of all, it was a period of longing to be back at home and wondering how my imaginings of family life would match reality.

Dakota Camp
The Dakota Camp was a collection of huts with a jungle airstrip about 2 miles distant. It wasn't much of a camp – just rough huts in a vast area of jungle and farmland – but it accommodated the blokes from the train and, wonderfully, we were free there and beginning our journey home. To me it didn't matter that I went straight from isolation on the train to a hastily put together isolation area within the camp or that only one afternoon and part of one morning were spent beyond barbed wire in my fortnight at the camp. What mattered was that I had my life back. I could glimpse a future.

There was a celebratory feeling in the air. For the first time since 1941 I celebrated my birthday: I was twenty-six on 4 September and prepared a not-so-tender chicken with various herbs and spices for a group of us. One of our patients celebrated his birthday with a sake party. Several bottles were brought in from a nearby village, poured into a clean metal bucket with fanfare and ceremony and scooped up by the mugful by happy patients.

119

The sole purpose of the Dakota Camp was to get blokes to Rangoon. Recovering prisoners and internees and setting up a physical Allied presence in camps started after the Japanese formally surrendered on 2 September. The recovery didn't happen immediately in the remote camps. For the first few days, all essential supplies like tinned food and quinine, as well as useful things like razors, blades and soap, were dropped by parachute from massive transport planes flying low over the camp.

It was a luxury to get new blades. My blades had finally given up the ghost after we left Bangkok. Captain Marks had given me some of his old ones, which did work a bit, but I normally let my beard grow and paid Johnny Bull five cents to shave me with his army knife that he kept honed to a razor's edge.

To be inundated with food was a blessing that is difficult to imagine after long drawn-out famine. Thousands of tins of food were parachuted in, some incorporating self-heating technology. We tried to eat heartily at first but couldn't tolerate a high fat diet or eat too much because our stomachs had shrunk. I remember being as sick as a dog after eating frankfurters in what I thought was gravy but turned out to be some kind of oil. After a little experimentation, we ate sparingly from the tinned foods and ate very little from the cookhouse, which was turning out large quantities of rice and meat and vegetable stew. It was all too much too soon, but so wonderful to know that food was available and that we had a choice about what we ate, how much and when.

By the middle of our first week at the camp, a Dakota brought in a small force of British Infantry and the British officer who had led elements of irregular Thai forces. They symbolically disarmed a unit of Japanese Infantry camped near the airstrip. There were other armed Japanese soldiers still in the area, but the gesture pleased our blokes, though we didn't see it, being in quarantine. The British Army then formally assumed control of the Dakota Camp. Weather permitting, more or less daily flights by a single Dakota followed: supplies were brought to the camp from Rangoon and thirty to forty blokes were taken out on the return trip. The camp's population fell quickly.

Being stuck behind barbed wire while blokes were going to Rangoon was hard on the nerves both for medics and patients. The patients sat around playing cards, wondering when they would get out of isolation. We medics weren't overwhelmed with work and wondered about the same thing. We kept a watchful eye on the smallpox contacts but they were all doing well. We continued to dress ulcers and treat malaria and dysentery cases. Blokes coped remarkably well with mild malaria and dysentery because morale was so high. There were some serious cases that required careful attention, but not many.

When we were not doing medical work, we talked endlessly about being free. It was such a great joy and so unexpected. We couldn't get over it. It was like a miracle. There was no feeling of bitterness about the war. It had happened. We were safe. We were going home.

We also talked endlessly about the future – about jobs, about life after the war and about our families and hopes. Dr Marks said he was looking forward to going back to his medical practice in Northern Ireland. Like everyone, he was thankful it was all over. He'd had a huge responsibility, especially on the march through eastern and central Thailand. Sammy wanted to go back to his old job as a quarryman in Meltham, West Yorkshire. He wanted a good stable job, a good family life and a few mates. Sid's dad ran a fish and chip business in Norwich and he wanted to join it. It was solid and safe. Bill Graham wanted to leave the Regular Army, return to the Northeast, settle down and get married, but wasn't sure what job would best suit him. It's a pity he didn't become a doctor. I said I'd return to my old job as a cost accountant with the West Yorkshire Road Car Company but wasn't sure I'd stay. I wanted something that was secure and reasonably well paid. Iggy didn't open up much about what he wanted except, like all of us, he craved security.

We talked at length about what post-war Britain would be like, and particularly the implications of the newly elected Atlee Labour Government. I think we all welcomed the change. Churchill was hugely respected but somehow represented the past, whereas the establishment of the welfare state and the new government's solid commitment to jobs appeared to represent a future in which British governments would avoid the mistakes of the inter-war years. There was no support for radical change. One bloke, who was a communist, droned on about the dictatorship of the proletariat. He was given short shrift and told to go to Moscow.

We talked in general terms about families and our hopes for relationships, but left unspoken our real thoughts about those we loved, perhaps because everything was so uncertain and we didn't want to

121

tempt fate by painting too rosy a picture of how wonderful life was going to be. I talked about being poor before the war and how I intended to use my gratuity and back pay so that the family could live better. I so much wanted to make up for the lost years. Others talked in a similar vein. We all agreed that the family that had sustained us during the years of captivity must stay together or at least stay in touch.

Looking back on it, this was always more of a great hope than a realistic aspiration. Very soon we were scattered around the British Isles with no real prospect of meeting up: distance was such an obstacle. Today, people might drive 100 miles a day to work and think nothing of it. Then, it was equivalent to going on your annual holidays to Redcar or Scarborough.

We didn't talk much about the past, but there was a great deal of interest in the British-led force that had shadowed us on our mystery tour through eastern and central Thailand. Some blokes not in quarantine met the officer who had led the shadowing force and passed on the news to us. We learnt that various groups of prisoners had been shadowed in Thailand in the final weeks of the war; that the Allied High Command had expected the Japanese to attempt to execute us at some stage; and that our forces were prepared to intervene at the first signs of a massacre. This news sparked lively discussion in our group. None of us ever had the sense that we were on a death march. I don't think this ever crossed the minds of the railway engineers or of the frontline troops who guarded us. But how would they have responded to a direct order to exterminate us? Soldiers, by and large, obey direct orders, however reluctantly.

After a few days at the camp, a British doctor and team of four or five medics arrived from Rangoon. They immediately took over all medical aspects of the camp from Dr Marks and our team. They were so different from us. The difference went far beyond their white coats and scrubbed appearance and our scruffiness. They exuded a busy professionalism whereas our professionalism was slower paced and informal. Like us, the new team soon realised that the smallpox contacts posed very limited risk of spreading infection, but still insisted that we remain in isolation, though this attitude softened towards Dr Marks and his medical team. We were told we could leave the camp because regular airlifts were about to terminate and were warned not to mention nursing smallpox patients to authorities in Rangoon because we'd go straight back into isolation

122

and get the relieving team into trouble. We'd worked that out for ourselves.

We washed meticulously in disinfectant, put on shorts and shirts that had been brought over earlier in one of the Dakotas, burnt our old clothes, and gathered together our few belongings. Next morning, Dr Marks, Sammy, Iggy, Sid Browne and I strolled the couple of miles to the airstrip: Bill Graham left on the next plane. It was a pleasant, carefree walk. In all, around forty blokes climbed on board. The Dakota pilot set off down the airstrip, but aborted the take-off because there was too much weight at the back of the air-craft. The weight was redistributed; the pilot started down the runway again and just cleared the trees at the end of the airstrip. We were on our way to Rangoon. It was the 16th or 17th of September.

Rangoon

Rangoon was the clearing centre for POWs and internees flown in from Burma, Malaya and various parts of Thailand. There were tens of thousands of us wanting to go home quickly and not enough available ships. The war had ended so suddenly. Shifting from planning the invasion of Thailand and seaborne invasion of Malaya to locating, concentrating and repatriating prisoners and internees – and at the same time dealing with their disparate needs and re-quirements – must have been an organisational nightmare.

On arrival, ladies from the Women's Voluntary Service showered us with bread and butter and tinned pineapple chunks. They were the first white women we'd seen in nearly four years. Responding naturally and easily to their bouncy, good-humoured kindness was a challenge and revealed, perhaps for the first time, the difficulties that awaited us in readjusting to 'normal' society.

After a few minutes we were loaded onto trucks and taken to a British military hospital. We were assigned to an empty ward that had steel-framed beds, proper mattresses and crisply laundered sheets that were tucked in with great precision. We were pleasantly surprised. It was like being brought to the Promised Land. Having hot running water and showers was an even greater surprise and was pure luxury. Having no doctors or nurses also was surprising. We were there for the best part of a day and night but had no visitors apart from a sailor who wandered in and gave us an army water bottle full of very strong rum. It was almost like treacle and had to be watered down. I don't know where the sailor came from.

123

He wasn't a patient or member of staff, but his gift was greatly appreciated as we settled down to play cards.

A sergeant arrived next morning and told us to get our kit and bunk down in some large empty shops on the other side of road from the hospital. While doing this I saw many blokes from the Cross Keys Division and decided to catch up with Sergeant Harry Jackson from that division. He was my brother-in-law, the best man at my wedding and a very close friend. After some searching around, I found out that he'd been shot accidently by one of his own men. I was never told the full story – the Army was sensitive – but it seems he was shot in June 1944 by a young soldier who'd been in action, woke up in the middle of the night thinking he was still in action, reached for a revolver (the first chamber was empty as part of standard operating procedure) and shot Harry in the head, in the process making a widow and depriving two young children of a father.

After a few days we were moved to a large British transit camp. We were exposed at last to all the outward trappings of western civilisation. It's amazing just how quickly one slips back into using familiar things as if nothing has happened in the intervening years. Food, once at the centre of our thinking, was banished to the periphery amid plenty and variety. Adjusting to a western diet, or the stodgy army version of it, didn't take too long, perhaps because we were young and had started the process at the Dakota Camp. Eating large helpings took longer. I continued to eat sparingly and carefully.

Having toothpaste was a novelty and so much better than using coconut husks but it was special only the first time. After that it was just accepted as a normal part of life. Having a decent haircut rated well above toothpaste. In prison camps I shaved my head or cut my hair very short to guard against lice. In recent weeks I'd started to grow it longer and now had the luxury of visiting a real hairdresser for a stylish 'short back and sides'.

I was issued full tropical kit. It was strange at first being in a smart uniform and I kept looking at myself in any mirror that was handy. I was a human being again. I wasn't an animal wearing rags. Wearing decent clothes gave me a huge psychological lift.

Using a knife and fork was the single most thrilling and important trapping of western civilization for me. I'd always hoped to use them again from my days at Changi. Then the association was with eating solid food because I was very hungry. Now the association was with going home.

Many blokes handled the tedium of the transit camp by going around Rangoon to see the shops, watch the street life and enjoy the entertainment – principally drink and sex. A few blokes had gone with Thai women while we were prisoners but restrictions within the camps and the greater restrictions on sexuality imposed by poor diet largely ruled it out. Now the local sex trade experienced a bonanza. The medical authorities issued warnings about the dangers of going with local girls because the supply of condoms couldn't match demand, and scores of blokes were infected with various venereal diseases. The names and descriptions of girls to avoid were circulated.

I had no interest in exploring Rangoon after finding out about Harry's death. My close mates also were not interested and our group held together tightly. We were habituated to camp life. We were safe there and well fed and had the opportunity to catch up with friends we hadn't seen for some time – blokes like Jock Lynas, from Kanchanaburi, and the voluble and likeable Captain Gotla, who we hadn't seen since Changi. Sadly, I never saw close friends like Nightingale and Proudlove: the last time was at Kanchanaburi Aerodrome Camp.

The camp provided an opportunity to start catching up with the world as perceived by the British Army. We were shown numerous films and newsreels about the war: films made at Ealing Studios in London about gallant men beating the Hun; Ministry of Information documentaries about battles and victories; US military footage on the war in the Pacific; and footage on the fire-bombing of Tokyo and the atomic bombing of Hiroshima and Nagasaki.

We were shown a plethora of films and newsreels on current affairs, particularly the post-war face of Britain and the emerging international landscape. It was the sort of material that would have been showing at British cinemas at more or less the same time and was interesting up to a point, but it never came close to answering the questions that worried us: How were we going to fit in to this new post-war Britain, and how would it influence or shape the next stage of our lives? No one was on hand from the military or elsewhere to provide answers or offer perspectives. Probably no one knew.

The tedium of the transit camp – the waiting, the form filling, the newsreels after the first dozen, and the limited repertoire of new hit songs – left plenty of time for discussing the future and what was going on around us. The only thing that was clear about the future, as our talk went round and round in circles, was that we hadn't a clue about it. The thing that mattered most to us – families and relationships – was the thing we could talk least about once the platitudes had been said and repeated for the umpteenth time.

My inner circle of friends was as close as brothers but how can you talk about very personal things when you can't match vision and reality in your own mind, and how do you deal with the heady mixture of optimism, pessimism and uncertainty that exists within the group? Some blokes knew that life was likely to continue more or less as before. Sammy had received a beautiful letter from his wife at the Kanchanaburi Aerodrome Camp and knew all was well. Sid, on the other hand, received a letter in Rangoon from his fiancé telling him she'd married somebody else. And I hadn't received a letter from Marion during the POW years. Many blokes were in my position. But how do you interpret this? You knew that mail deliveries to the camps were uncertain and that Japanese distribution of mail, once received, was idiosyncratic. You also knew that relationships could wear out.

Our discussions at this time started to reveal an 'us' and 'them' mentality in relation to our liberators. This distinction had first struck me when the new medical team arrived at the Dakota Camp but it became much stronger at the transit camp. I saw the British Army there. It wasn't the army I felt I belonged to. I felt quite a stranger. I was comfortable with ex-prisoners but these other soldiers could have been from another planet. This sense of disconnection is difficult to explain but we were different men for having been under the Japanese: we felt different and believed the new lads looked at us as if we were different.

Some of these perceived differences were no doubt fanciful, the product of overworked imaginations trying to interpret quizzical looks and comments. Many of us wondered whether we were being blamed collectively for the surrender of Singapore: we were the failed soldiers and they were the victors. I'm sure this was part of the explanation in some cases, but doubt whether it can be generalised. Blokes who'd been fighting hard through Burma a few weeks earlier weren't likely to indulge in useless intellectual retrospection.

More likely, some of the 'us' and 'them' mentality reflected our wariness and suspicion of those beyond our group. We'd adapted to a hostile world by drawing on the strength of the group, with all its inner and wider circles, and these new people weren't part of it. But, frankly, we were different. The new lads dressed more smartly than we did. We were still slightly scruffy in our new uniforms, perhaps because we were so used to wearing rags or were just looking forward to leaving the Army. They looked so much younger than we did. I was only in my mid-twenties and they might have been in their early twenties, but we were in some respects a generation older – a quirk of war compressing experience and time, as well as the physical effects of prolonged starvation and three and half years of captivity under harsh conditions. They were fitter, more active and seemingly more alert than us. Their 'fat' faces glowed with vigorous health. And they did things differently to us. It wasn't just saluting and marching about and the fact that we'd forgotten about drill and weren't interested anyway.

There'd been massive technological changes in the years while we'd languished as prisoners. The Army was more mobile and methods of doing things, whether in medicine, transport or working with weapon systems, had evolved tremendously. The lads in that new model army were more confident and more assured of their skills than we'd been. We didn't belong to that army. We imagined ourselves as a separate army or, more accurately, in no army at all. Perhaps even before going to Rangoon, I no longer saw myself as a soldier and neither did my close mates. That was all over.

SS *Chitral*
Managing daily frustration was my dominant memory of Rangoon. Like every other ex-POW, all I wanted to do was go home as fast as I could, and all that seemed to happen was to be told to go here and there, only then to be told to wait somewhere else for further instructions. Essentially, I was free to wait for something to happen like a good, disciplined soldier: the Japanese had taught good discipline, so I waited. I also pretended to be fit and resolved not to have my right foot and leg X-rayed in Rangoon. There was significant ligament damage but I wasn't going to provide the authorities with any possible excuse to delay my return to England, so I said nothing.

I watched for my name on ships' lists and then watched as closely for what was happening to my close mates. Several ships left Rangoon for England during the time I languished in the city: the *Worcestershire* on 18 September, the *Boissenvain* on the 20th, the *Indrapoera* on the 23rd, the *Ormonde* on the 26th, and the *Orduna* on the 29th. Juggling expectations and hopes with daily disappointment was nerve-racking. I was like a small child waiting for a Christmas that never seemed to get any nearer.

My name at last went up on the repatriation list against the SS *Chitral*. I would be leaving for home on 2 October. With great relief, I went through the hundreds of names and discovered that Sammy and Sid – the blokes who'd been closest to me in Thailand – would be on the same ship, as would friends like Len, from London, and Jock Lynas. Sadly, friends like Bill Graham were going home on other ships as, I suspect, were men like Dr Marks, Dr de Soldinoff and Dr Gotla. Officers had their own cabins and areas to walk in, but they weren't snobbish men and would have made contact if they'd been on board.

The *Chitral* was a liner that had been converted into a troopship. It was not especially large at 15,000 tonnes and the 2,200 passengers were packed in tightly. The vast majority were ex-prisoners, along with a small contingent of former civilian internees. The cargo hold was hot, smelly and cosy and had been partly transformed by new technology. The hammocks that had been a feature of our outward voyage from Greenock so long ago had been replaced by multiple rows of yard-wide canvass – three tiers high – that were secured to steel scaffolding. A quart could indeed be poured into a pint pot.

The mood on board was buoyant and happy. Sailing conditions were excellent until we reached the Bay of Biscay: the ocean was like glass for much of the way. There were pleasant sea breezes and days passed contentedly wandering around the decks, sitting and talking, and watching sunsets, dolphins surfing on the bow wave and the antics of flying fish. There was no medical work to do. I never saw the medical staff but they couldn't have been very busy. The seriously ill had been kept in hospitals in Rangoon and Singapore or had been repatriated on the first ships to leave for home.

The food was substantial: I'm sure the authorities were using the voyage to fatten us up. We had bacon, eggs and sausages for breakfast; beef stew or steak or pork chops and solid puddings for lunch; something similar for dinner; snacks to fill in the edges whenever we wanted them; and cans of condensed milk and meat for other times when we might be hungry. It was, of course, impossible to be hungry, which meant that blokes took home plenty of canned food, which was probably the point of the exercise. I must have put on nearly a stone during this period. When I arrived back in England, I weighed 115 pounds compared with 147 pounds at my first Army medical inspection in late 1939.

Perhaps the only irritant on the voyage, and it was unavoidable, was that we kept stopping at different ports to pick up mail and ship's supplies. In normal times this would have been a highlight of the voyage but it seemed to conspire to delay our homecoming. We stopped off at Colombo for a day or two, which gave everyone an opportunity for sightseeing and buying presents. I bought a 24-carat gold ring, exotic confectionery for my daughter and cartons of cigarettes.

The next stop was Suez. We didn't stay long, only getting off the ship to board buses that took us to a massive warehouse that was overflowing with full khaki winter kit, every other imaginable form of British military apparel and thousands of pairs of Army boots. An hour sorting through these things added another bulging kit bag to be lugged about. In some respects it was ridiculous getting an additional uniform because almost all of us were on the threshold of leaving the Army, but we were heading into winter and we were still part of the British Army, so there were good reasons for it.

We stayed in the docks at Port Said and stood off Gibraltar to pick up mail and ship's supplies, and then headed for the Bay of Biscay. Conditions there were appalling. A storm raged; the ship was tossed about; and the Government's force-feeding policy was interrupted. I staved off the worst effects of seasickness by vigorous deck walking with my pal Len. The storm raged as we approached the English Channel. Perhaps eighty or ninety per cent of blokes were badly seasick and, one day out of Southampton, there was no general excitement at our homecoming.

The storm abated somewhat by the time we saw The Needles. Everyone, including those who had retreated to their berths, came out on deck, pressing together on the port side to gaze at the coast, and home. For a moment or two this imperilled the ship, which canted dangerously, and the captain ordered us over the tannoy system to disperse. Southampton came into view. It was early on Sunday 28 October. It was cold and wet but mercifully no longer windy.

Arriving home

As we berthed, flags were flying; there was bunting everywhere adding a splash of colour to the grey day; a military band played the National Anthem and lively ditties like *I Do Like to be Beside the Seaside*; and hundreds of people crowded the docks. There were relatives, friends, dockers, troops, and perhaps curious people happy to watch the spectacle. People were shouting out as they saw their loved ones. There was cheering and frantic waving. School children were waving Union Jacks. It was a fantastic scene. There was nothing contrived about it. There was just genuine happiness, relief and excitement.

I felt very emotional and the hairs on the back of my head were standing up. I was back in England but it felt foreign. I saw no familiar faces. I felt neither joy nor relief. I just felt strange. I never discussed this with anyone because it was so odd. I should have been over the moon with happiness. I can't fully explain my reaction. Maybe it was coming face to face with an uncertain future. Fantasy had been part of surviving. Now it was going to be tested.

Once we docked, various dignitaries came on board briefly. A general read the King's message over the loudspeaker system and an alderman from Southampton Council welcomed us on behalf of the city. It was all over in a few minutes and the speeches, such as they were, were easy to miss amid the bustle and chatter. And then we disembarked: there were lines of men wearing greatcoats against the winter's chill, thankfully not having to wrestle bulging kit bags because two men from the Pioneer Corps had been allocated to each of us to do that. We disembarked quickly and ladies from the Women's Voluntary Service stuffed our pockets with chocolates, cigarettes, buns, and apples as we passed by. There was no time for talking or for cups of tea and cakes. We just kept on moving towards the buses that took us to the transit camp on Southampton Common.

The camp was like a small city that provided accommodation, copious quantities of food and entertainment over a two or three-day period, and attended to all the necessary but tedious administrative details of immediate resettlement in England. We had chest X-rays, received part of our pay and were deluged with documents ranging from railway warrants to ration cards to clothing coupons to application forms for voting. Rail journeys to our home towns were organised, lost property claims were filled out, campaign ribbons and service chevrons were stitched onto uniforms, welfare officials dealt with missing wives, kind souls advised us not to exert ourselves and take time getting back to normal, and telegrams were sent out to families providing details of arrival times.

Apart from the hustle and bustle of the transit camp and the nagging thought that it was yet another stumbling block in the way to getting home, it is memorable for two reasons. The first is that there was no medical examination (at least as far as I can remember). If there was one, it must have been very perfunctory, which seems odd given that virtually every one of us had suffered from major diseases at one time or another during the years of captivity. I had to wait until late November or early December to have a medical in Leeds. The belated medical reminded me of the medical prior to recruitment. Various doctors and specialists poked and prodded me and after half an hour pronounced me to be in excellent health. Whether they really understood anything about tropical diseases beyond standard textbook accounts was by the way. There was no psychological examination. It beggars belief that most blokes wouldn't have come back with some form of post-traumatic stress but this was ignored, probably because it was assumed that service-men would put the war behind them and get on with things, which is what I tried to do.

The second is that the Army made a genuine attempt to discuss future job and career options. Presumably drawing on briefings prepared in Rangoon, a group of officers proposed that the Army would arrange for me to study medicine if I so wished and would pay for a five-year degree course. I explained that I had not considered this option and could decide on next steps only after seeing Marion and my daughter Diane. I was not really attracted to the offer, generous though it was. I'd never had any expectation of going on to sixth form or to university – that was unimaginable pre-war, given the costs involved – but my real reason for not pursuing the offer was that I didn't want to be away from the family for another long period. I should have realised that the Army would have paid for a flat for us.

After the transit camp, my group of mates largely broke up. In some senses the fabric of my personal life was disintegrating and I was more apprehensive than ever. Fortunately, Sammy was still with me and on 1 November we travelled together to Waterloo Station in London and then by Army truck to King's Cross. We were the only ones getting off at King's Cross and the lads chucked down our kit and drove off. We stood outside the station waiting for something to happen. Perhaps we were waiting for an order. It dawned on us that we were on our own and had to think for ourselves. I don't think either of us liked it. We were uncomfortable and a bit lost, but this was the first time I fully comprehended that I was free and that the essence of freedom is having the confidence, motivation and initiative to make one's own decisions about what to do and where to go at a time that suits you. Before that moment, all those decisions had been made by the Japanese or, more recently, by our own authorities. Freedom is one of the hardest things to adjust to.

We had rail passes for Yorkshire and boarded the Leeds train. An entire carriage had been reserved for Far Eastern Prisoners of War and we had it to ourselves. Strangely, we didn't know what to talk about. There was no point talking about the past because we'd lived it together and the future was an unknown to varying extents for both of us. Sammy repeated what he might be doing and I repeated what I might be doing. We agreed to keep in touch. But, for the most part, the journey passed in silence.

Sammy and I got off at Leeds, he to take the train to Halifax and me the train to Harrogate. Parting was very hard for both of us. By this time it was late and I boarded the last train to Harrogate, man-handling, as best I could, my two kit bags, cartons of cigarettes and assorted presents. The train was full of servicemen and only one seat was unoccupied. The lads were very kind and picked up my kit and stowed it in the racks. I was again struck by how young they were. I was pleased they didn't ask me anything. The bloke sitting next to me was obviously an ex-prisoner from Thailand or Burma and wanted to talk about the rough time we'd had. I think he wanted to tell the lads how he'd suffered. I had no intention of sounding like a martyr and kept silent. I was relieved when we arrived at Harrogate Station. It was just before midnight. I was the only person getting off. The lads helped me with my kit.

I had imagined my homecoming so many times laying awake at nights over the years. I had pictured arriving around mid-afternoon, being met by many people, being embraced, and seeing familiar streets and blue skies. The reality was different. I was met by

Marion, my three youngest sisters – Jesse, Florence and Doris – and a testy stationmaster telling me it was very late and to hurry up so he could lock up. It was nerve-racking for Marion and me. There wasn't much opportunity to say any thing as we were ushered out of the station. I said something banal like 'Hello Marion', and she said 'Hello Ken, you're back'. Later she commented that I had big eyes, perhaps because my face was still gaunt. I think I commented that English people seemed to have big cheeks, because I was so habituated to seeing gaunt faces.

It felt like a reunion of strangers, as indeed it was. I'd effectively disappeared with the fall of Singapore. My frantic telegram, sent just before the surrender, didn't get through. Neither of the two 'tick a box' postcards I'd sent – one from Changi, the other from Kanchanaburi – was received. Marion didn't know whether I was alive or dead until September 1945. And both she and I had gone through an intense period of personal growth and development. We were different people.

There was one taxi in the station forecourt. Marion and I took it and my sisters walked the couple of miles to our parents' home on King Edward's Drive. I got out there and Marion continued in the taxi with the kit bags to our home at 23 Gordon Avenue. It was wonderful seeing my parents and sisters again. In the early hours of Friday, 2 November, I walked back to our home. It was a lovely feeling to be back. My daughter Diane, who was now five years old, was in bed and I went to see her. The poor child was woken up. It must have been very confusing for her being hugged and given presents by a strange man in the middle of the night. My in-laws welcomed me but there was no time to talk. It was late and my father-in-law, Len, had to go to work. Later that day, I went with my young daughter to my parent's home: they had baked a large iced cake emblazoned with 'Welcome Home'.

Chapter 10

Confronting Reality: Adjusting to Family Life

Re-settling was difficult for all returned servicemen and women, their families and communities. War changes people and societies. It separates families and communities for years. It allows people to do things and see things that would be unimaginable in peacetime. And, when it's over, it creates massive adjustment challenges for families as they try to rebuild relationships and a 'normal' life, as well as for whole communities as they struggle to cope with profound economic and social changes.

I don't think the scale of the problem has ever been estimated for veterans and their families of my war or the Great War. Partial estimates have been made for later wars: for example, the Australian Department of Veterans' Affairs estimates that around twenty per cent of Australian Vietnam War veterans have post-traumatic stress disorder (PTSD) – a persistent condition known as shell-shock in the Great War and, more commonly, war neurosis in my war.

I have no way of proving it but being Far Eastern POWs probably meant that the scale of PTSD was higher among us than for servicemen as a whole (and perhaps far higher than suggested for Vietnam War veterans), and that it was harder to make adjustments to changing circumstances in families, the workplace and society more generally. We were catapulted from citizen soldiers to slaves, who didn't know if (or when) our captivity would end. We briefly became citizen soldiers again and then returned to being citizens in normal society. Effectively disappearing from the world for over three years meant that the amount of catching up with families was greater than for servicemen and women who'd been able (more or less) to correspond freely with their families. Coping with freedom was strangely taxing. We were powerless and then suddenly had the power to make our own decisions. It may seem odd but, at least for a time, freedom felt uncomfortable, even frightening. And the albatross of defeat still hung around our necks: there are no medals for defeat. We were blamed for the biggest defeat in British military history. People asked the legitimate question: how could a smaller force of Japanese beat us in Malaya and Singapore. I suspect many people in Britain didn't think much of us.

Health issues among Far Eastern POWs were more serious across the board than among returned servicemen and women generally – a fact demonstrated by our substantially higher mortality rates through the second half of the 1940s and 1950s. Psychological problems also were significant. These days when soldiers return from tours in countries like Iraq and Afghanistan, there is a strong focus on trauma counselling. We never had that and many POWs spent years revisiting their traumas.

The British Government was aware of these problems. Towards the end of the war, it commissioned research into the problems of rehabilitating POWs. A string of confidential papers were produced, now on the public record, that identified risks of increased aggression, quick violent tempers, resentment of and cynical contempt for authority, and feelings of alienation. The Government also was aware that these risks would be highest among Far Eastern POWs. After the war, the Government produced reports analysing the difficulties faced by POWs in returning to civilian employment, cataloguing frequent job changes, high rates of absenteeism, alcoholism, and aggression. In more recent years, evidence has accumulated in this country and overseas on Far Eastern POWs' relations with their long-suffering families and less long-suffering employers. It confirms the expectations of Government psychologists in the mid-1940s.

The Government helped to ease resettlement problems to a small degree. There was a legal requirement that service personnel could return to their old jobs and there were superficial medicals that demonstrated that the great majority were in good physical health. But, in fairness to the Government, it's easy to understand why getting a 'demob' suit and some help with finding a job was about as good as it got and why returning service personnel were substantially thrown onto their own resources and those of their families. In the early post-war years, Britain was the most heavily indebted nation in the world. Orderly planning for the labour market was impossible given the millions of returning servicemen, the hundreds of thousands of munitions workers going back to civilian occupations and the dislocation between production and markets. The Government probably hoped resettlement problems generally, and problems with POWs in particular, would sort themselves out, which they substantially did.

Dominant memories of family life

Memory is a very selective process, particularly about families. Selection makes the past more understandable or less painful, or both. What I remember most about the first weeks and months of being home is how wonderful it was to have a real family again; to be young, safe and sound and in reasonable health; and to do things spontaneously. The smallest things pleased me – to walk around familiar streets; to look at the shops and houses; to see normal human beings with fat cheeks wearing proper clothes. It was a joy and confirmation that I was free. At times I couldn't believe it. Above all in the immediate post-war years I remember the renewal of the strong relationship with Marion, having a good time – holidays, wining and dining, and buying good clothes, and our family's general good fortune.

Making up for lost time

Marion and I took off the November and December of 1945 and went all over together. It was a holiday to rekindle the vitality of our relationship, share youthful pleasures and rediscover the lost years. The 1946 hit song, *To Each His Own*, expresses how we both felt towards each other. The lyrics are still powerful:

A rose must remain with the sun and the rain
Or its lovely promise won't come true
To each his own, to each his own
And my own is you
What good is a song if the words just don't belong?
And a dream must be a dream for two
No good alone, to each his own
For me there's you

CHORUS
If a flame is to grow there must be a glow
To open each door there's a key
I need you, I know, I can't let you go

136

Your touch means too much to me
Two lips must insist on two more to be kissed
Or they'll never know what love can do
To each his own, I've found my own
One and only you

For many months, having a good time was a far higher priority for us than finding good jobs. We were optimistic. We weren't thinking about the future. We wanted to enjoy life and had the money to do it. I had over £300 from my Army gratuity and back pay covering the period from the fall of Singapore. It was a significant sum and would have been a sizeable deposit on a house, but we wanted to live well and not skimp and save for an uncertain future. Together with my wages, when I rejoined the West Yorkshire Road Car Company at the start of 1946, and Marion's wages from the War Agricultural Executive Committee, we had more than we needed and spent up to the hilt. We'd never been so well off.

The gloom and drabness of immediate post-war Britain didn't register with us. Mid-week we'd go to the pub. It was pleasant on a summer's evening to walk up Bilton Lane to the Dragon. Marion drank gin and tonics in those days. At weekends, we went to Leeds. For the first few months this was the ritual almost every Saturday, but over time it lengthened to every two or three weeks. We'd look around the shops and then have lunch at the top of Lewis's store. We'd listen to the orchestra and Marion would usually order lobster thermidor – her favourite meal at that time. Going to the cinema was standard fare. On some Saturdays, we'd go to the cinema in the afternoon, then have tea and cakes at Betty's Café and go back to the cinema in the evening. On Sundays we'd sometimes go out to country pubs with friends who had a car.

We spent a great deal of time shopping for good clothes. I needed a new wardrobe. I didn't have much pre-war clothing and what I had was sold during the war to eke out the family budget. There may also have been an expectation that I was dead. For the first time in my life, buying good clothes was a high priority for me. I took pride in my appearance, perhaps as a reaction to the POW years when I'd dressed in rags and to the pre-war years when I could only afford the basics. Getting good clothes wasn't hard if you had the money and the ration coupons, and I had both – the Army issued me with ample clothing coupons.

Marion and I picked out a new wardrobe. I remember going into Kitchen's menswear shop, on James Street, in Harrogate. Someone had ordered a three-piece made-to-measure suit in a beautiful light-weight woollen material. They hadn't collected it and it fitted me perfectly so I bought it there and then. I bought clothes from Allan's, near the Prospect Hotel, including a light green Egyptian cotton shirt with a matching yellow silk tie. I was told they were for display purposes only, but I wouldn't accept that and bought them. I bought tailored sports jackets, matching trousers and bespoke shoes. It took time and effort to get fine clothes, but it was worth it. I even picked out an elegant 'demob' suit. It was grey with a pale white stripe and looked quite sharp: it wasn't the typical blue, grey or brown three-piece suit.

Marion has always liked beautiful clothes and she bought some stunning outfits during this period. Half the population may have been shuffling about in respectable but worn clothes from the 1930s – these were the austerity years – but that wasn't for us, or Diane. Smart children's clothes and shoes were scarce, but were available if you had the money.

We also had money for holidays. Going abroad would have been inconceivable. Even going down to the south of England would have been an adventure, but the playgrounds of Yorkshire were very accessible. We were especially fond of Redcar. In May 1946, we took Diane for a week's holiday there playing miniature golf in Zetland Park, walking along the sands to Saltburn and escaping the chilly North Sea wind by playing pinball in an amusement arcade where we were about the only customers. The prizes were bobbins of different coloured cotton. We still have them and must have paid a small fortune for them.

We had a fortnight at Redcar staying at the Coatham Hotel – the best hotel in the town – in the summer of 1947. Marion then stayed on for another fortnight by herself. She hadn't any authorised leave and was subsequently sacked by the War Agricultural Executive Committee. But the weather had been good and she wasn't thrilled with the job: costing feedstuffs used by livestock farmers was about as exciting as watching paint dry. Clerical work for women was plentiful and not encumbered by community ill-feeling towards women doing 'men's' work. She quickly found a new job as office manager of a company distributing slot machines to upmarket hotels.

My gratuity and back pay went down fast and were exhausted by the summer of 1947, but this didn't stop us from having a good time. Marion's wages would have been half or two-thirds of a man's wage for doing the same job and our combined wages weren't especially high. But we saw no reason to change our lifestyle and didn't think about saving for the future until 1948, when our son Michael was born and Marion joined the Inland Revenue Service. A second child forced a sense a responsibility. I was nearly thirty.

Good fortune

The family was fortunate in some key ways in the immediate post-war years. Marion and I were getting on reasonably well. We had a beautiful, healthy and very bright little girl and a baby son. My physical health was good – I was thin but otherwise fine. So many POWs came back in a dreadful state, like one poor fellow who lived near my parents: he'd been through Changi and the camps in Thailand and died shortly after the war from a range of tropical diseases.

We lived well, basically because of generous support from my in-laws. The war had touched them the least among our extended family. They gave us a roof over our heads at a time when one-fifth of the British housing stock had been destroyed by war and when private rental accommodation was both scarce and very expensive. We lived rent-free, paying only for food. We had our own living area, coming and going as we pleased. Len was easygoing and Lill did everything for us. She was resourceful, creative and hard-working, and kept the household going. She had numerous contacts and, despite rationing and the general shortage of meat and eggs, always produced wholesome and nutritious meals.

We were under no pressure to move into alternative accommodation. Marion didn't want to leave her parents' home. Diane was happy there. Len and Lill were especially keen for her to stay. I alone was open to leaving. We were offered alterative housing – a 'prefab' at the beginning of 1946 and a council house near Harrogate General Hospital a few months later – but continued to stay. It was convenient and living rent-free meant we stayed for much longer than we otherwise might. Lill looked after Diane, which was important because Marion and I were working, and then also after Michael. It wouldn't have been possible for Marion to continue working with

139

two children in our own home. We didn't think of buying a house until the early 1950s.

Difficult memories

In some important respects, readjusting to home life is difficult to talk about. While blessed with good fortune we inevitably faced tough times. Some families may have adjusted seamlessly to their pre-1939 ways, but I doubt many did. Perhaps older men slipped back into well-established relationships, secure in their own homes, but even for them it couldn't have been easy reconciling changing expectations, forging relationships with older children and juggling home and work responsibilities. For younger people who'd effectively grown up in the war and were starting out from scratch and living with in-laws, the challenges were daunting. In our case all the perceived certainties underpinning family life had changed: I'd changed, Marion had changed and Diane was unrecognisable.

The combination of war and my time as a POW changed me fundamentally. Like so many others who went to war and were exposed to the wider world, I grew up. The Army introduced me to alcohol and tobacco and showed me how to convey meaning with a reduced vocabulary: I swore all the time, no one took offence and it took a great deal of self-discipline to remove the worst profanities.

I lost my strong religious convictions. I attended two services at my old Four Square Gospel Church in York in late 1945 or early 1946, but it was not the same. The cheery hymns, music and oratory were the same but all the young people I'd known prior to the war were scattered around Britain or were overseas. I never went back to Pentecostalism or anything else. It felt 'normal' for my wife and me to lead a secular life.

I was uncertain where I fitted in to the general scheme of things, at least for the first few months. Pre-war, I knew: I was a grammar school boy who'd got there on his own merits; I had a reasonable, though uninspiring, first job; I was married with a child; I felt I was going places. In the immediate post-war years, I struggled to fit in to the family and at work, and for a time found difficulty in talking naturally and confidently to people I didn't know well. Social gatherings of one form or another became a standard part of our life – part of having a good time – but I didn't like them even with Marion at my side. I felt almost alone in a roomful of people. I wasn't different from them on the outside – I was wearing good quality clothes, better than most – but I was tongue-tied and floundered and felt a complete stranger. I'd never go into a pub by myself, fearing someone might talk to me and I wouldn't know what to say.

I also was aggressive. I hadn't noticed it so much pre-war, though I have a natural arrogance, but I was aware of it in the early post-war years. Trying to live the Christian life and meeting confrontation by turning the other cheek were things of the past. They'd been part of my upbringing and acquiescence was a necessity in the POW camps: blokes had to have a death wish to show their true feelings to the guards. But once I returned to England, suppressed feelings of anger and frustration rose to the surface and were directed at full force at those I considered were trying to oppress me. I couldn't just flick off a switch and move on. I had a lot of the POW left in me. I tried to expunge it but something as simple as the smell of fish conjured up memories of washing ulcer patients' dressings, started my heart racing and made me sweat and want to retch.

My frustration and anger came out most strongly in the work-place (Chapter 11) but spilled over into family life, manifested in a tendency to view life in black and white terms. I sought order and predictability, which made me insufferably stubborn at times and unwilling to compromise, even on some trivial things. Emotional frailty and my need for empowerment after so many years of being powerless may explain some of the stubbornness.

My immediate family changed as much as I did. The war transformed Marion from a beautiful and vibrant girl into a more beautiful, vibrant and very determined, hard-working woman. She had grown up fast. She'd had to. Seventeen weeks after Singapore's fall, the Army had the cheek to terminate her spouse allowance of a few shillings a week on the presumption of my death. As a plucky nineteen-year-old, she had the guts, determination and nous to take on the Army bureaucracy and have it reinstated. This perhaps was the beginning of her rapid transformation into a modern, liberated woman of the war generation.

Like tens of thousands of other young women who found out they were neither wives nor widows, she had some hard choices to make. She could put on widows' weeds, be dutiful, knit socks or dig for victory and possibly miss out permanently on youth; or she could claim her youth, grow up fast, take a demanding job because she couldn't live on the Army pension and have her mother, Lill, look after our daughter. She opted to join the Air Ministry, which (along with other London-based ministries) had moved part of its operations to Harrogate. She earned good money, was increasingly self-reliant and assertive, developed a sophisticated social life, and emerged from the war years full of confidence with the world as her oyster.

Diane was a mystery. I last saw her when she was eighteen months old. Now she was a five and a half-year-old child. She didn't know me. I was just somebody who appeared from nowhere. It was difficult for the two of us to bond. To her, Len was like a father, not a grandfather, and I suspect she regarded Lill as more of a mother than a grandmother and Marion as more of a big sister. Lill basically brought up Diane. She and Len adored her.

We had to sort out a workable balance between Marion, Diane and me – it couldn't be all beer and skittles; I had to accept some degree of drift in the relationship with my parents and sisters; and tensions in the relationship with Len and Lill had to be smoothed out.

Relationship with Marion

My solid relationship with Marion was tempestuous at times. To some extent this was driven by our different personalities. Marion wasn't a 'homely' person like my sisters. She was the mistress of her own destiny. She was exciting, complex, high-spirited, difficult, fierce, highly social and instinctive. She was like Vivien Leigh's portrayal of Scarlett O'Hara in the 1939 film *Gone with the Wind*. I was more clinical, introspective, stubborn, and aggressive. The mixture could be toxic. Neither of us knew the meaning of being patient with each other.

To a much larger extent in the immediate post-war period, the difficulties we faced reflected the fact that we were comparative strangers and had changed so much. I was nineteen going on twenty when we married; Marion was seventeen going on eighteen. I was more edgy, moody and autocratic, and Marion must have struggled to come to terms with the differences. She also had been transformed by the war years. She enjoyed her youth, freedom and opportunities for experimentation, but this came with baggage, or perceived baggage, which challenged my mother and elder sisters' late Victorian values. It also, frankly, posed problems for me. Yelling matches were frequent and on one occasion resulted in physical violence when I pushed her into a china cabinet. She could have been hurt but the only damage, fortunately, was to some ornaments.

I'm enormously proud of Marion and admire her gutsy approach to grasping change and personal growth in the war but was mystified by it at the time: it wasn't what middle class girls from Harrogate did. The compromise we struck didn't always work but it worked well enough for most of the time. I didn't discuss my POW years with Marion and the rest of the family because I felt awkward doing so and they weren't interested. Conversely, Marion didn't discuss her life in the war or any other aspect of the war with me. It was understandable from both points of view. Both of us wanted to move on. Why rake up things that make us uncomfortable? We developed the art of tiptoeing around sensitivities while pretending everything was perfect. I pretended to be psychologically the same as I was before becoming a POW. Marion pretended the war didn't happen.

Relationship with Diane

The relationship with Diane was inevitably going to be difficult. No one at any age wants their life to be turned upside down, especially if they have no control over outcomes. For Diane, I probably existed as a black and white photograph or as a vague concept. Now I, a total stranger, turned up. Why should she accept me? What did my arrival imply? Could it imply leaving the home that she knew and where she felt secure for a strange new home? Would she see her grandma and grandad again? This was all very frightening. My homecoming and the months that followed must have been testing for her.

From my point of view, how do you bond instantly with a stranger? I knew nothing about raising children, but felt I had to be involved. This, of course, is a minefield where actions, wise or other-wise, can be interpreted in a variety of ways by the child and others. There were a range of views on how to bring up Diane and I wasn't the sort of person at that time who wanted to depart too far from preconceived notions: the world was still black and white. I wanted to live the fantasy of family life as I'd imagined it in my POW years and that had sustained me through that bleak period. The fantasy had focused on the first few minutes of my arrival at the railway station, and never came true, but beyond that I'd imagined an idealised family where the years were no obstacle, everything was

143

wonderful and we were secure. That was my greatest hope. Reality would never match fantasy.

Sorting out the pieces and moving towards a new equilibrium took time for both Diane and me. I'm not sure we ever reached that equilibrium.

Relationship with parents and sisters

My wife's supposed path to perdition during the war raised eyebrows and assaulted the values, religious instincts and prudery of my mother and elder sisters. They had no time for Marion – she was the Scarlet Woman of Babylon – and she had none for them. The wider family drew apart, though with the wonderful plasticity and self renewal of families, elements came together again over the years.

The first signs of tension were present at the welcome home party organised by my parents. Marion wouldn't go to the party so I went with Diane, having received clear instructions not to stay for dinner. This was understandable because it was my first full day back home and, equally understandable, my parents and sisters wanted Diane and me to stay. There was a lot to discuss. My mother, in particular, wasn't especially interested in hearing about my POW experiences – my survival was the result of the family's prayers and the Lord's work and that was that – but she was interested in discussing Marion's 'goings on'.

I came to see less and less of my parents and sisters. I went to some family gatherings, but their views about Marion created friction, which was best avoided. My drift away from formal religion and my 'hedonistic' lifestyle also were issues that emphasised the gulf that opened up between us.

Relationship with the in-laws – Lill and Len

Lill and Len saw their small house shrink. There were now two households, and in one of them there was noise, continuous smoking, drinking and gambling – mainly poker and sometimes strip poker. Len neither smoked nor drank, but gambled on the horses. He came down with a nerve rash towards the end of 1947 and Marion developed a 'nervous condition'. I left briefly around this time to live with one of my sisters.

My obsession with food was a constant irritant. Britain at the end of the war wasn't a land flowing with milk and honey. I couldn't tolerate waste, then or now, but I saw it everywhere, and my efforts to curb 'wasteful practices' caused friction. I also protected 'my' milk and 'my' vegetables from the predations of the in-laws. It was silly but the threat seemed real enough at the time. In the destructive and pointless way of arguments, disputes over food sometimes escalated, dredging up things best left to quieter and more thoughtful moments.

Conclusions

Re-integrating families, nuclear and extended, takes time and effort, is awkward and outcomes are unpredictable because there are so many gaps and areas of rawness in the intertwining relationships. Steering a course through the family crosscurrents was taxing for all concerned. For me, the journey underlines that experience shouldn't be confused with maturity. Marion and I now had plenty of life experience, but none of it really helped to handle the pitfalls of day-to-day family life. In my case, I'd broadened my experience beyond anything I could have anticipated a few years earlier. But what had that experience taught me: it had taught how to survive as a slave worker among mates who provided mutual support. It hadn't taught how to fit more comfortably into 'normal' society or how to establish an easy and comfortable relationship within the family. That side of me hadn't matured at all. If any thing, it had just been snap frozen while society at large and the family had changed and evolved. I think Marion was in broadly the same situation. She had grown immeasurably during the war, but not necessarily as a mother or homemaker.

The two of us just had to get through the ups and downs as best we could and reach the other side. We succeeded as a family because Marion coped with an argumentative, food-hoarding husband; I learnt to bend a little; and, most important, we loved each other, warts and all.

Chapter 11

Disconnecting with the Community?

Unlike cities such as London and Liverpool that had been transformed by heavy bombing, places that I knew best, like Harrogate and Leeds, were just slightly run-down versions of what they'd been in 1939. Bomb damage was minimal in Harrogate and wasn't too severe in Leeds: both places felt instantly like home. But beyond the bricks and mortar and the public gardens, they had changed, just like the rest of Britain. The pall of austerity with its ration books, overcrowding, making-do, and shabbiness hung heavy if you chose to focus on it. There was a sense of pessimism, particularly among people of my father's generation. They looked back at the previous war and feared the worst – unemployment, poverty and another war (this time with the Soviet Union). My father was convinced that peacetime, for however long it lasted, would be as testing as wartime. Even the weather seemed to test us. The winter of 1947 was the worst in living memory.

Among younger people, I suspect, the gloom was relieved by a liberal dose of optimism. Certainly in my case, optimism was anchored in the almost magical developments of 1945. The slaughter had ended. At the beginning of the year, I was marching through the jungles and paddy fields of Thailand and was resigned to a short life of servitude to the Japanese. By the end of the year, I was home and had my life back.

Old men might drone on about history repeating itself and the need to endure yet more hardship, but I wasn't enduring austerity. After the conditions I'd been living in, there was nothing drab about Harrogate or Leeds. I was making up for lost time with Marion. Life was good. The worst I had to put up with was the petty dictatorship of shopkeepers, who initially were loath to sell me cigarettes because I hadn't been one of their regular customers. Of course I hadn't. I'd been in a POW camp. Having to explain myself to these tyrants was galling.

My challenge was fitting back into Britain. I'd lived by certain rules in the camps: veil your emotions, keep yourself under control, respond to circumstances you can't change, draw on the strength and support of close mates. I stepped onto a train in north central Thailand that brought me to the Dakota Camp, took a plane to Rangoon and then boarded a ship bound for England to live by another set of rules: be open, engaging and comfortable with a range of people, including those you hardly know. That transition is hard for anyone. For me, the security of belonging to a tight group, even under dire conditions, was replaced by a sense of exclusion from post-war life. The worst effects persisted for at least a year. Problems with reintegrating into the workplace persisted for years.

Easing back into the community
In those early months what could I say that was of general interest? For a time there wasn't much interest in even talking about the war in Europe, North Africa and the Atlantic. Blokes who'd been in the services, of course, did talk about it but, by and large, people wanted to put behind them the interesting war I'd missed – and that I wanted to know more about – because at that time they were coping with building a new life in a new world.

Part of me wanted to talk about my war, at least to convey that it hadn't been a holiday camp and that we'd done our bit, but in the broader community there was virtually no interest in the war in the Far East and in POWs of the Japanese. There were occasional stories in the press about Japanese atrocities, the camps and proceedings of war crimes trials in Tokyo and Singapore. Newsreels provided graphic images of brutalised men in the work camps. Some parents wanted to understand better how their sons had died. But the public at large were happy to forget about Singapore and Southeast Asia. Perhaps it's human nature to forget about defeats. Certainly public indifference reflected the fact that the great majority of the population had no stake in a faraway war that was remote from their daily lives. Their war had ended with Germany's surrender.

147

In these early post-war years I never had an in-depth conversation on Far Eastern POWs*. If it was touched upon by chance, someone might observe that being a POW must have been a daunting experience before moving onto something more interesting and topical. Occasionally, someone might note the harsh conditions in the camps, perhaps embellishing with their own stories of personal hardship in the war, such as being unable to get fresh eggs or buy new clothes or, more credibly, coping with the loss of loved ones. Thinking about the supposed hardship of rationing makes me laugh now, but sixty-odd years ago it made me squirm. The average person had no concept of conditions in Southeast Asia and there was no point in enlightening them. Discussing relative levels of hardship would have been pedantic and made me look like a fool or a martyr, and I had no wish to be seen as either.

The general lack of interest in and understanding of the Far East left me feeling as if I had nothing to say. I was a misfit. I can't describe the feeling adequately. It was like having a hole in the middle of my life that prevented me from engaging with people in a relaxed way. How do you fill such a hole? How do you forge networks and friendships and mix easily with people again? The answers weren't obvious to me then or now.

It took a good year before I started to feel more comfortable with people and much longer before I fully regained my pre-war self-assurance. Support from the family was important in building confidence but at least as important was support from a group of young people at the War Agricultural Committee. The hole in my life remained – there was so much that couldn't be talked about – but somehow this was skirted around and became less of an obstacle as friendships developed with people who generally hadn't been in the services (some were too young), were comfortable in the present and accepted me as I was. They helped me to move on with less introspection and critical self-analysis. Bit by bit there was more to talk about and the past became a less demanding master.

---

* Interest in Far Eastern POWs spiked briefly in the late 1950s with the release of the film *The Bridge Over the River Kwai*. Colleagues and friends were especially interested in the possible factual basis for the actions of Colonel Nicholson, a fictional character who collaborated with the Japanese in constructing the bridge. The film was not authentic but was highly enjoyable. My favourite part was the blokes whistling *Colonel Bogey*. That was realistic.

It would have been sensible to reinforce these new friendships with links to old mates from the POW years. Keeping the network together had been so important in Rangoon and on the ship coming home. But for me, it went up in smoke after repatriation. There was a brief flurry of meetings in the first few weeks: a group of mothers organised a reunion dinner for six Far Eastern POWs in the Harrogate area at the Black Bull near Kettlesing just before Christmas 1945. Marion and I stayed the weekend with Sammy and his wife and attended a POW dinner in Sammy's honour at Meltham, near Huddersfield. Sammy was the only Far Eastern POW in the village. They treated him so well. There was a wonderful atmosphere of supporting friendship. Marion and I also met Sammy two or three times in Leeds. It was always good being with him – a meeting of brothers. We didn't talk much about POW days. We talked about current things. I never met Bill Graham again, the man I'll always regard as the best of the lot of us. To this day, I regret not attending his wedding in Tyneside.

The Leeds branch of the Far Eastern POW Association was established in 1947. The branch membership must have been substantial because many Yorkshire lads had been captured when Singapore fell. I deliberately didn't join it, foregoing the comradeship and the opportunity to meet people to discuss not only our common past but also our adjustment to post-war life and the future. I shut out the past, at least during the day: it returned at night when I couldn't sleep. I knew the importance of human relationships but it's hard sometimes to apply commonsense understandings in a complex world. I couldn't have both my real family and the POW community. I chose Marion.

Going back to work

I thought that going back to work as early as I could was the key to accelerating reintegration into the broader community. It was, to a considerable extent, but the passage wasn't as easy as I'd expected. I didn't have to worry about getting a job. The Reinstatement in Civilian Employment Act meant that I, along with tens of thousands of others, went back to our old jobs. It was perhaps the best thing the Government could have done for us and revealed that political leaders had learnt some lessons from the aftermath of the Great War.

In January 1946, three months prior to being demobilised, I returned to work as a cost accountant at the West Yorkshire Road Car Company – the company I'd joined after leaving school ten years earlier. I didn't hesitate in making the decision. I'd enjoyed the job before the war: it had been permanent at a time when jobs in the Harrogate area were scarce; I liked working with numbers; some of the older blokes were qualifying as chartered accountants; I liked my colleagues; and, while wages were modest, I was happy. I thought it might work out for me in the post-war years.

I rode my bike up Skipton Road to work as before; I sat at the same desk; I even worked on files I'd left at the beginning of 1940. The senior staff hadn't changed, but there'd been a massive turnover of junior staff, the people I'd worked with. All the fellows around my age had left and been replaced by girls who'd been telephonists and retail assistants before the war. They were complete strangers. I was supposed to belong but was on my own.

I felt abandoned. Being an individual in the workforce was unsettling after the close support of mates in the camps and the stability of POW society. But it was more unsettling that these strangers were earning more than me, although they knew little or nothing about bookkeeping and cost accounting. I knew this for a fact because the company's costings hadn't been calculated during the war years – there was no one to do the work – so my first big job was to compile the data. That meant seeing a broad range of company records, including confidential material relating to the salaries and wages of all staff. I was consumed with resentment towards those girls.

A hard thing to accept – and it wasn't the fault of the company – was being treated as the office junior again. I'd matured in some ways and handled life and death issues. I wanted to be treated as the person I'd become, not as the boy who'd left for war. I objected to being told what to do and how to do it by the haughty young girls who were technically my bosses. And I reacted predictably when the office supervisor – an officious man working in Dickensian style at a desk that was raised slightly on a small stage – called out to me 'be quiet down there', as if I was a naughty child in primary school. My crime was talking to some young women. I told him where to go in plain army language. I really detested this treatment. Even now it makes my hackles rise to think about it.

The hardest thing to accept was senior management's lingering contempt for me as a conscientious objector at the start of the war and possible perceptions that I hadn't done my bit for the country by languishing in Japanese POW camps. In my own mind, any residual element of shame at being a conscientious objector had been removed working in the camps as a medic. I wasn't one of the 'friends of Hitler' as the press had portrayed conscientious objectors or someone who'd joined the RAMC for an easy life where I could rob my wounded comrades. I wasn't a coward. I'd proved myself as a man. All this, I thought, was now being questioned. All the loathing I had for the Japanese and the resentment I harboured towards authority in general erupted at a short meeting with management to discuss wages. They wouldn't raise my wages to reflect war service. I gave a week's notice and left. I lasted a little over one month in the job.

Getting a job may have run second to having a good time but was still essential. Like almost everyone who'd been through the turbulence of the inter-war period, a large part of me craved for certainty and security. I remember all too clearly the hand-to-mouth existence of coal miners and their families during the General Strike, foraging for coal on slag heaps and being fed on bread smeared with meat paste supplied by local charities. I recall also how in later years my family's fortunes moved above and below the poverty line in accordance with my elder sisters' earnings and the intermittent earnings of my father. He left the pits in 1927 with a lung disease that would have killed him had he stayed.

A large part of me also wanted more income and to get ahead. In the week or so following my departure from the West Yorkshire Road Car Company, Marion and I considered taking over a bakery in a mining village near Castleford. It was tempting. The business was thriving but the coal industry was in turmoil over future plans for nationalisation. There were strikes and rumours of strikes. Miners naturally would have expected a line of credit from village businesses when money wasn't coming in and, naturally, to pay off debt at their own pace when times improved. We didn't proceed.

A much safer option was to become a temporary clerk at the War Agricultural Committee. I applied, was hired and subsequently took the Civil Service examination to become a clerical officer. It was good to join the Civil Service. Agriculture sounded interesting and varied, especially in comparison with options like the Post Office

Savings Bank. The job became permanent and, importantly, wages were higher than in my previous employment. They were around £4 per week, which was more or less the national average at that time. A good wage would have been £6 per week.

Over a few months I developed some friendships and my sense of being an outsider lessened, but I continued to confront authority. I was bitterly against what I perceived as arbitrary authority. Some of this anger existed pre-war, but back then you had to be subservient. You played the game because it was a dreadful labour market.

In a restrained way I continued to bridle at 'authority' during my Army days. Much of the discipline seemed petty, arbitrary and at times ridiculous and I was fortunate to work as a medic under liberally-minded doctors. Most Japanese and Korean guards provided an object lesson in the abuse of authority and I emerged from POW life determined never to allow anybody ever again to walk over me. I wasn't going to be subservient, least of all to blokes who'd never gone to war, had reached exalted positions without passing exams and were drawing fat salaries. A few knock backs combined with a measure of natural arrogance produced a lot of aggression that didn't win friends or influence people, at least in any positive way that helped my cause.

I loathed and detested those fellows who'd taken over during the war when there was no one to challenge them, and who were instructing returned servicemen in how to fit in. My immediate boss at the War Agricultural Committee was a former stores checker from the West Yorkshire Road Car Company. He'd always dressed formally in a dark suit, wore a bowler hat and carried a briefcase. I used to pay him his wages and had joined other lads in kicking his hat about the office. Another minor boss had been a bus driver on the Harrogate-Leeds run. I'd paid his wages over a period of roughly five years but he acted as if he didn't know me. Yet another had been a milkman, who'd become a tractor driver (and was therefore exempt from the call-up) and became a district agricultural machinery manager.

To some extent I had a bee in my bonnet about being a grammar school boy who, in the normal course of events, could have reasonably expected to advance rapidly on the basis of hard work and application but, as it turned out, got stuck at the starting gate for a while. But more broadly, my exasperation with the new order reflected the general astonishment of returned servicemen at having to start at the bottom again, and the sickening impact of bosses occasionally boasting about their strategies for avoiding the call-up.

It took some years to moderate the resentment and aggression and start playing the game with nous and a measure of maturity. When I did, my career took off.

Overall, the past remained difficult territory for me but the disconnection with the community faded as I developed new friendships, built confidence and genuinely started to engage with people. Feeling more settled in the community was the key achievement of these years. I was disappointed with my jobs. I spent too long feeling aggrieved with bosses, minor and important, and fighting my own silly war against them.

REFLECTIONS

Chapter 12

Surviving as a POW

I attribute my survival to a great deal of good fortune, a bare sufficiency of food, effective medical assistance, good comrades supporting each other, positive practical thinking and, ultimately, when life started to hang in the balance towards the end of the war, living only for the day.

The role of fortune
I was remarkably fortunate to survive. The gap between surviving and becoming a mortality statistic was very small. I could easily have perished on the same Japan-bound convoy as my pal Robbie or during the bombing of the Bangkok docks or on the march through eastern Thailand. The march by the main party, which followed us from Nakhon Nayok in eastern Thailand to Phitsanulok in the centre, was designated a war crime by the Singapore War Crimes Commission in July 1946. A Japanese captain and *gunso* received long prison sentences for their treatment of prisoners. The sentences seem harsh if their behaviour was no different from our guards', but the Commission's finding that POWs were starving, had no medicine and were deteriorating rapidly was accurate.

I was especially fortunate never to become seriously ill because, once moving down the slippery slope of illness, it was so easy to become broken and helpless and reach a point where personal willpower or the miracle-making of clever and dedicated doctors were incapable of clawing back what passed for health and vigour.

Of course, I didn't see myself as particularly fortunate at the time. I only saw the daily struggle to survive – my own and others. Looking back on events, good fortune was a key factor, maybe even the main factor, in my survival (and perhaps the survival of most men) because so many of the variables affecting life and death, such as the lottery as to the camps you were sent to, and when, and the jobs you were allocated, were beyond any individual's control.

I went to several camps and, in each one, we all worried constantly about food, but there was a margin of subsistence, at least for most of the time. This was the critical difference with distant work camps at the end of supply chains: there the margin often didn't exist. Prolonged starvation produced disease, and disease accounted for the great bulk of POW deaths. Eastern and central Thailand were different stories: starvation tested my resolution to keep plodding on more than any other time as a prisoner.

Getting the right job in camp was vitally important. Heavy labouring jobs with limited access to food and medicines were the worst. Among other ranks, cooks and truck drivers had the best jobs and survived better than most because they had access to food. I'd never accuse cooks of stealing food and overeating but I never saw a thin one! Drivers for the Japanese had an opportunity to scrounge food if they were driving food trucks. Their mobility allowed messages to flow between camps and their endeavours were rewarded with food or cigarettes. Drivers, naturally enough, struck up relationships with their Japanese or Korean guards and could expect cigarettes and perhaps food if they got on reasonably well.

I was fortunate to be a medic. Medics did die, but mortality rates were very low compared with rates prevailing across Thailand. We had easy access to available medicines, knowledge of hygiene and training in keeping fit, and we were part of a supportive network of people doing mostly agreeable, important and challenging work that kept us motivated.

Beyond fortune

Beyond good fortune, perhaps the single biggest factor in my survival, and the survival of so many others, was the miracles performed daily by camp doctors. The work of men like de Soldinoff, Marks and McDonald to create so much out of so very little was the really heroic thing to emerge out of the tragedy of POWs in the Far East.

Mateship in all its forms was the other notable positive that emerged from the tragedy and helped to mitigate its scale. Mateship was not unique to a country or particular group but friendship and mutual inter-dependence and reliance were part of the elemental glue that kept men alive and functioning through the ups and downs of captivity. In my experience, mateship evolved slowly over time. In the early days at Changi we tended to have a group of good friends, in my case mostly from Yorkshire and the Northeast, and beyond that friends and comrades from the 198th Field Ambulance. By the time we arrived in southern Thailand, almost everyone had a special mate at the centre of their wider networks of good friends, other friends and acquaintances. At the same time, military units that had held together in Changi became looser: at Kanchanaburi, I was part of a medical team whose members came from a mixture of units. Specific military groupings were, to some extent, replaced by a loose sense of mateship or camaraderie among prisoners. Blokes didn't need to know each other well, or even at all, to share the same fears and hopes and, in some indefinable way, to rub along together.

While the form of mateship evolved, its core remained un-changed. Close mates were like family. They ate together and slept in the same part of a hut. They owed their primary loyalty to each other. Fears about food or existence could be faced with those who shared things and had unspoken understandings of each other's needs. Mates improved the odds on survival: isolation did the opposite. If you lost your best mate, you had to get another one fast.

Fear was manageable during the day. Night was the danger time when we were lying on our sleeping platforms like sardines in a row, and yet were as alone as we ever could be. It was dangerous to think too much about wives and families. I sometimes thought that Marion might be watching the same moon as me. I'd think of the time difference and what she might be doing at that moment. I wondered if she'd be thinking of me. I thought of all that silly non-sense and much more besides. But longing for home and wonder-ing about the future and worrying about the separation and the not knowing were agony if they went on and on. They made you desperate, banished sleep and didn't resolve anything. I craved contact through letters but this didn't happen and doubtless would have been a two-edged sword anyway. A letter would have brought joy and been read and re-read countless times. But it also would have focused the mind on happier times and places and made the present harder to bear.

I couldn't stop thinking about home in the first year or two of being a prisoner. It might happen at any time but times like wedding anniversaries and Marion and Diane's birthdays were always difficult to handle. You would think of what they might be doing and when (and if) you'd ever see them again. Christmases weren't nearly so bad because we always tried to do something to make them a bit special. But after a while, I tried not to think about home. I didn't dare. I longed for it so much.

This transition was part of a broader change in my thinking and approach to life. Faith ceased to be a central part of my being. In the early months at Changi, I naively saw captivity as my trial in the wilderness, and hoped it would make me stronger and better able to talk with understanding, conviction and authority about life and religion. Being the only son in a large evangelical family, I probably still harboured ill-formed ambitions to become a lay preacher. By the time I was at Kanchanaburi, I had a much looser view of God and His works. I didn't blame Him for the situation we were in. I didn't torture myself with mealy-mouthed rubbish about why God was allowing this misery to happen. But for reasons I don't really understand, I just gradually reached the point where I didn't think a great deal about Him, and faith wasn't central to my survival. I knew plenty of blokes who travelled in the reverse direction. It's impossible to generalise about these sensitive and highly individualistic matters.

I tried to keep focused on the positive, practical things of life: what I was doing at work; little things that added something to the day; what I might be doing with mates; things that were going right in my life.

This meant doing my best each day as a medic to make a difference to people's lives and then accepting the loss of patients, even friends, as a fact of life. This wasn't being callous. I felt I couldn't afford to grieve too much for the dead: it didn't do them any good but inner turmoil harmed me, and the dead bloke could be me next week or next month.

It meant doing my best not to surrender to misery, hate, anger, discontent, regret, and avarice because they weaken you and make you vulnerable. What's the point in hating the conditions – the guards, the dysentery, the slow starvation, the physical wretchedness? It just created frustration and anguish. And what's the point in worrying about rights and wrongs and issues of justice? It didn't get you anywhere and could be dangerous if living in your mind started to isolate you from mates and lessen the focus on practical day-to-day imperatives.

160

Most of all, it came to mean not living too much in the past or the future. I had been fluctuating between believing that the war must end soon and thinking that I'd be stuck in Southeast Asia forever. But sometime in the second half of 1944 I started to push thoughts of home and freedom into the background. This wasn't being disloyal to anyone. I was just trying to simplify my ambitions and desires, and concluded that it was safer for me not to put my hopes in freedom because it might never happen and I didn't know how I would handle the disappointment. It was easier to live day-to-day, accepting the possibility of remaining a prisoner for forever and making the best of it. Freedom, if it came, would then be a wonderful bonus.

I can't really say whether others started to lose hope in a better future. It was too personal and I never discussed it in much detail. But I found that accepting the reality of the present was easier to deal with than to give way to the emotional highs and lows of the rumour roller-coaster in Thailand. There was so little firm news about the outside world. Senior officers had access to hard information through secret radios, which operated in all the base camps, despite the death penalty for operating them. Big news stories like Germany's defeats in North Africa and Russia, the invasion of France and American progress in the Pacific would have been known after a brief time lag by a select few within the camps. There were excellent reasons for holding such information tightly: the *Kempeitai* were always searching for radios fearing subversion, sabotage and rebellion. But the policy did impose a burden on the vast majority of other ranks who were outside the information loop and had to rely on rumours and ad hoc information brought in by drivers and working parties.

By mid-1945, our isolation in eastern Thailand was so complete and our knowledge of the outside world so minimal that I was convinced the war would drag on forever. Some blokes had picked up a jumbled message from the Thais in May or June that the war was over, meaning presumably that the war against Germany was over. But even if we believed this, it was an unimaginable leap to assume that Japan would capitulate soon. The Imperial Japanese Army was tenacious and skilful; the Japanese were deeply entrenched in Southeast Asia and eastern China; and we were in the middle of it. If it were possible to defeat Japan, I thought it would have happened by now.

At this stage I could either sink into despair and hopelessness or accept things as they were. I was not going to sink into despair and hopelessness. I banished thoughts of freedom and home because the longing was too distressing and was a distraction from getting through the day. There was no such place as home. I was going to survive, and that meant having some cigarettes and stretching my rations as far as they'd go.

It's amazing how focused your thinking becomes when the margin of subsistence starts to thin. You focus on the moment – you are hot, exceptionally hungry, very tired; your foot is a mass of pain; you are thirsty and can't get boiled water for tea. You don't care about what's around you – the colours of the jungle, the sky if you can see it. You are consumed by getting through the moment and then the day. You endure. You think about food, keeping 'healthy', staying alive. Mates help you. You help them. You do your job by instinct. The future barely exists.

That's how I got through it.

Final thoughts

In my view old men can't congratulate themselves too effusively on their survival skills as Far Eastern POWs. I was either very fortunate or, as my mother said, God looked after me because she prayed so hard. I can't discount divine intervention but I put a great deal down to being fortunate in the way events unfolded.

I knew a handful of blokes who gave up and died but most hung on to life tenaciously. Some blokes, in a terrible state, wanted it to be over, and who could blame them. But even shambling wrecks overwhelmingly wanted to live and struggled to survive against the odds. Endurance has its limits – truly amazing ones – but physical reserves are not limitless. In the end the body runs down so far that loss of life becomes inevitable.

I've never been troubled by why I survived and so many others didn't. I've never felt guilty and I've never searched for reasons beyond good fortune, a bit of extra food, good mates, and taking a day at a time. I've never attributed my survival to some grand strategy of my own devising. If there was a strategy, it was a simple one of getting through each day and hoping for eventual freedom and, when that hope seemed too threadbare and distressing in its unattainability, accepting life as it was and making the best of it.

Chapter 13

'Yellow Little Bastards': Evolving Perceptions of Race

As a POW, I never discussed generic attitudes towards the Japanese and Koreans with close mates. It's not the sort of thing you discussed at the end of a hard day. We'd talk about the 'yellow little bastards' did this or that or discuss strategies to avoid particular individuals on working parties but we didn't intellectualise the bastardry.

I doubt whether too many blokes spent time actively thinking about possible links between the actions of some rotten individuals and their race, though the link existed in the form of crude national stereotypes. Any British child growing up in the 1920s and 1930s was taught at school, and perhaps at home, to hold the King's enemies in contempt. The culture of accepting the pronouncements of 'superiors', whether parents, school teachers or the Army hierarchy, meant it was easy to swallow the nonsense that the Japanese were small, short-sighted, cruel, untrustworthy people, lacking in the dependable personal, business and organisational qualities of the British.

The fall of Singapore shattered part of the myth. No one could doubt the organisational skills and determination of the Imperial Japanese Army. But much of the mythmaking remained intact through the war years and limped on into the 1950s and 1960s: propaganda can live with you for a long time.

It took me years to break the association between race and myth and see the tragedy of the POW years as a consequence of the aspirations of the narrow, brutal and power-crazed clique that controlled Japan through the 1930s and first half of the 1940s.

Hatred as a POW
Even as a POW, it was obvious that the Japanese military system underpinned our mistreatment. The discipline system seemed to be

based on superiors bashing so-called inferiors. Officers and *gunsos* bashed their underlings for almost anything: for not carrying out an order or not carrying it out quickly enough or with enough spirit or for making a tiny mistake or in some way irritating a bad tempered 'superior'. We were the most inferior and so were bashed the most.

There were vicious guards who indulged their warped fantasies in the perfect environment provided by the camps. Inevitably, I focused on them and that coloured my impression of the whole. But there were others I came to know to some extent who were reasonable enough, did their duty to the best of their ability, hoped to go home in one piece, and had no pretentions of being Asian supermen.

Hatred doesn't encapsulate my attitude to Japanese and Koreans guards. Some odious individual might kick me, give me a back-hander, beat me up, swear at me, or degrade me in some other way, and this would bring raw hatred to the surface. But hatred wasn't something that stayed with me because it didn't help me to survive. It did the reverse. It was a distraction from living. What stayed was resentment at being treated like an animal and frustration at our collective impotence to change things. Resentment and frustration gnawed at me in much the same way that hunger did. Like every-body else, I wanted to strike back at the injustice and oppression but couldn't. The stories of brave men standing up to the Japanese and Koreans and taking beating after beating are either false or the blokes concerned were very foolish or, in a handful of cases, were genuine heroes. No one in their right mind wanted to get bashed because some guards never knew when to stop.

When at last we were free, we were told that the Japanese were preparing to execute POWs following Allied invasions of Thailand and the Japanese home islands. Whether this assessment was true or not isn't the point. The point is it sounded plausible as a desperate last act to counter the possible arming of POWs by Allied paratroops and resonated with what we knew about the Imperial Japanese Army: soldiers were intensely patriotic and unswervingly obedient to the chain of command.

The spectre of possible mass executions could easily have kindled white-hot hatred among armed POWs and led to rampant personal retribution. It did neither. Once we reached the Dakota Camp and then Rangoon, we hardly talked about the Japanese and Koreans.

164

This had nothing to do with Christian values – forgiving your enemies – and everything to do with the sudden removal of oppression and doubt, the luxury of freedom and private dreams of home. At this time there wasn't much room for hatred or loathing. Blokes were generally content for the culpability of individuals and groups to be addressed by others at another time.

Attitudes over time

The tumultuous heart-warming joy of freedom inevitably couldn't last. Bit by bit, it was replaced by the daily grind of earning a living and the ups and downs of family life and, bit by bit, I started to loath my former captors. At the very least I developed an even more negative version of the negative national stereotype of the Japanese that persisted in post-war Britain into the 1960s.

It was easy to slip into this way of thinking. Simply perpetuating my own prejudices or the silly assumptions underpinning the national stereotyping of the Japanese required little or no effort compared with trying to make sense of my POW years. I also was in no mood at that time to reflect seriously on the experience. The POW years were a convenient excuse for some of the difficulties I experienced in readjusting to post-war conditions. Living in the north of England in the 1950s and 1960s I didn't see Japanese people in a business or social context and so had nothing to challenge wartime images. And, when I did think about the camps – or when memories seeped back at night – it wasn't pleasant because the awful bits crowded out the rest.

Sometime in the 1970s and 1980s my attitude towards my captors started to change. For the first time I wanted to place my worm's-eye view of events as a POW in a military and political context and read reasonably widely and watched as many documentaries as I could on the war in the Far East. Enough time had gone by and I was secure enough to look back. For the first time I also encountered Japanese people who had grown up in a liberal democratic environment. I was living in London during part of this period and regularly saw groups of Japanese businessmen and tourists and heard Japanese spoken. I also saw multitudes of smiling, well dressed and technology savvy young and middle-aged Japanese wandering around places like York. None of these people bore any resemblance to my mental image of Japanese from the 1940s. I particularly remember a group of Japanese coming to Ripley Castle, near Harrogate, in the early 1980s to demonstrate the finer points of the tea ceremony. It was the first time I felt no lingering animosity to Japanese people on account of race or some imaginary link to my treatment as a POW. I was just interested in what they were demonstrating and found I could interact naturally with them.

In a very imprecise way I started a solitary quest to re-evaluate my POW experience. The unpleasant images and sounds were still there, but there was room for pleasant memories. I came to accept that you can't tar a whole army or a whole nation with the same brush.

One consequence of seeing a more mixed picture was starting to buy Japanese goods. I test-drove my first Honda in the early 1980s and then bought ten over the years – Accords and Preludes. I also bought Japanese televisions, radios and stereos. They deserved their reputation for quality – they weren't the cheap and shoddy imitations once popularly believed – but I wouldn't have bought them if I'd still carried the mental baggage of the early post-war period.

A more important consequence was starting to think critically for the first time about the general rottenness of the POW years. The thing I hate most about that time is the utter pointlessness of deaths from malnutrition and tropical diseases. The vast scale of these deaths was the result of Japanese neglect and indifference to the welfare of prisoners at the highest levels of government and the armed forces, and the communication of that indifference down the chain of command. I can't accept that the high death rates were the result of Japanese inability to manage logistics or lack of awareness. Managing supply chains would have been challenging but Japan was technologically advanced and had sophisticated management systems. The Japanese leadership also must have been aware of the desperate state of POWs, especially of the skeletal men in the more distant work camps. Common sense should have told senior leaders that they could have achieved more from fit, healthy productive men. Food was plentiful enough in Southeast Asia if there had been the will to feed POWs adequately.

While there were bad individuals among the guards, our real enemy was the perverted political and military system that demanded conformity, didn't tolerate debate, imposed impossible burdens on its soldiers and wider population, and was indifferent to the suffering this caused its own people and others.

Hiroshima and Nagasaki

When I first heard of the bombing of Hiroshima and Nagasaki in early September 1945, I cheered along with the other blokes. We were delighted with this thing called an atomic bomb. We didn't understand what it was, but understood clearly enough that each of these cities had been destroyed by one bomb, the war was over, unbelievably we were free, and we were going home. I was amazed by the march of progress. Seeing jeeps for the first time in Rangoon was impressive but one bomb obliterating an entire city was technological progress on a scale that was hard to grasp. Mixed in with amazement was joy that my fate wasn't to be stranded forever in Southeast Asia and gratitude that I'd been saved from the very real prospect of dying from disease and starvation or from being caught up in ground fighting or being worked to death.

I honestly can't say I felt any sympathy for the tens of thousands of lives that were destroyed or ruined in those searing, dazzling blasts. Insofar as I thought about it at all, the deaths were easy to dismiss as payback for Japan massacring, enslaving and starving millions of people across Asia and the Pacific during the previous decade. I didn't see the dead as people, just numbers, and was oblivious to the irony that the Japanese military must have seen us in much the same way after Singapore fell – vast numbers of enemy soldiers to be used up as required.

Over the years I've never questioned the bombing and the continuing tragedy from the effects of radiation. I've never fixated on what the bombing brought in its wake: the potential for catastrophe from major power rivalry in the atomic age and, in recent years, the menace from well-resourced terrorist groups getting access to bomb-making material. I've also never felt guilty about it or become entangled in unanswerable intellectual conundrums: Would Japan have surrendered without the bombing of Hiroshima and Nagasaki given defeat in Okinawa, the blockade of the home islands, the threat of starvation, and the certainty of more devastating conventional bombing? Should the United States have informed Japan that it had a new weapon of awesome power and would use it if Japan rejected the demand for unconditional surrender as set out in the Potsdam Declaration? Should the US have invited Japanese officials to watch a nuclear test in the middle of some desert? Could the US have given the Japanese adequate warning of the cities

167

selected for destruction so that people might flee? Should the US have sought Japan's surrender after dropping one bomb?

For me, the justification for bombing Hiroshima and Nagasaki is clear-cut: it stopped the war or at least was a significant part of the reason why Japan capitulated so suddenly.

I attribute my survival to Japan's sudden surrender. Conditions in central Thailand had become desperate by mid-1945. If the war had dragged on for many more months, POWs' death rates would have soared from starvation and disease. It's anyone's guess what would have happened to POWs scattered across East and Southeast Asia if there had been long drawn-out fighting in Thailand, Malaya, Indo-China, and the Japanese home islands. At the very least, many POWs would have been slaughtered in revenge attacks or become 'collateral damage' as the ground war intensified.

Japan still possessed considerable military might in mid-1945 and controlled massive overseas territories. Defeating it conventionally would have meant prising it out of these territories and ultimately taking and holding the Japanese home islands. By helping to bring the war to a speedy end, the appalling devastation of Hiroshima and Nagasaki probably, on balance, saved many tens, perhaps hundreds, of thousands of lives on both sides.

Apology

I know that many former POWs, along with Japan's Asian neighbours, would welcome a frank apology on behalf of the Japanese nation for the imperial rampage through Asia and the Pacific in the 1930s and 1940s. Confronting what happened should be cathartic and preferable to perpetuating collective amnesia or compromising twentieth century history.

A formal apology may be a long time coming from this consensus-driven society, particularly given concerns that it could lead to a fresh wave of claims for compensation: £10,000 was paid to each former prisoner of the Japanese in the late 1970s. But even if it takes many more years, there is no excuse for Japan continuing to sanitise histories dealing with the inter-war years and the Second World War and for honouring war criminals as national heroes. Providing a straightforward understanding of Japan's recent past, particularly at school level, should be a basic right in a liberal democratic country. Telling history as it happened also might go some way in addressing the ambivalence towards Japan that still exists through-out East Asia.

Chapter 14

Enduring Legacy

I see my war service as being a prisoner of war of the Japanese in Southeast Asia. Serving as a British soldier for five and half years was largely coincidental. Prior to leaving for Singapore I was bound to a desk for much of the time, wasn't really a soldier and wasn't learning too much about medical work. The campaigns in Malaya and Singapore were real soldiering and, for me, were a brief and grisly crash course in providing emergency medical assistance. The more insidious and drawn-out campaign that followed against disease and oppression forms the most vivid period of my life when I became a medical orderly worthy of the name. The vividness of that time never goes, even though I've spent the greater part of my life trying to push its memory into the background. Memories come back in pictures. Even feelings of oppression and frustration come back if I think hard enough about some events, though thankfully they no longer come back unbidden.

In a very inexact way, I now divide my life into pre and post-POW years. Admittedly, much of what I am has little or nothing to do with the war or being a POW. My core values, like the importance of family, building for the future, avoiding waste, and shunning blatant materialism, were formed in the depression years of the 1920s and 1930s while living in a large family that moved in and out of poverty. My broad objectives in life – having a family, a pleasant home and garden and achieving reasonable affluence – have never changed over time. And my focus on practical matters, like facts and figures rather than aesthetics, literature and intellectual abstraction, has been part of my makeup since the earliest days.

But in other respects the combination of the war, being a POW and perhaps just growing up changed me in ways that would have been unimaginable for my twenty-year-old self in 1939. I went from being a closeted young lad, content to work in a job with few

169

promotion prospects and live a conventional northern suburban life in a fundamentalist religious family, into a man who'd seen the best and worst of people, had amazing experiences and wanted more out of life. I wanted to be back with my wife Marion, but beyond this I wanted to be respected in the community as someone whose contribution to the war effort more than negated the shame of being a conscientious objector at the start of the war, and to be recognised as having the drive and qualities to advance professionally.

Being a Far Eastern POW was a bad experience that I wouldn't wish on anyone. There were obvious costs at the time and significant costs and difficulties later in reintegrating into families, the community and workforce. To this day, there are gaps in my relationship with Marion and my daughter Diane that show up in occasional awkwardness and reserve. But from the safe distance of sixty-odd years, I know that, overall, I've benefited from being a POW. I'm privileged to have known true comradeship. The best friendships of my life were formed in the POW years and, in large part, account for my survival.

I'm proud of my contribution as a medical orderly to saving men's lives and feel privileged to have worked with doctors who were both fine men and real heroes in saving lives. I'm also privileged to have known men who will never be recorded as heroes but who performed amazing things like one lad from the Northumberland Fusiliers who had the guts and nous to 'relieve' the Japanese of everything from quinine to stethoscopes to supplement supplies at the Kanchanaburi Hospital.

I consider myself fortunate that the POW years made me tougher, more determined and more resilient. Now I'm the carer for Marion, who has dementia. It isn't easy and there isn't the same level of support for sufferers of this affliction that there is for those with other terrible diseases such as cancer. In some respects, accepting things that can't be changed and taking each day as it comes isn't too different from POW days. If the comparison is valid, it adds an odd symmetry to my life.

I'm also pleased that the POW years gave me some insights into human nature and life generally that perhaps depend on being tested in extreme ways, as I was on the march through Thailand. Four points are especially significant for me.

First, I was nearly always hungry as a POW but only experienced true starvation on the march through eastern Thailand. Emptiness

170

day after day gnaws at you and creates desperation. This is still the lot of much of humanity whose images are all too familiar on television. That this deprivation and desperation exists alongside the waste and wanton materialism in rich countries is obscene.

Second, we suffered as POWs because the Japanese military dictatorship drove generally decent people to do some awful things. This doesn't excuse the bastards who wanted to use every opportunity to bash and humiliate men and who were willing participants in a war of racial hatred and resource acquisition against the United States and China, as well as the old colonial powers. But those few Japanese and Koreans I knew best, and they were mostly privates, were ordinary blokes and, to some extent, were victims much as we were. They didn't conform to the stereotypes of the Japanese that so easily seduced us prior to the fall of Singapore and were substitutes for reasoned understanding.

We now have a lucid comprehension of the very different Japan that has emerged over the last sixty years. The pressing challenge now is to ensure that the seduction of 'sloppy thinking' doesn't replace reasoned understanding of current challenges posed, for example, by the rise of China and resurgent Islam. Clichéd responses will come at a considerable cost, as they did in the 1930s and 1940s.

Third, I lived in very close proximity to a wide cross-section of people, knowing them under stressful conditions that stripped away social graces and revealed true character. The standout impression for me is that people are both very fragile and very resilient. Lives can be snuffed out so easily but, for the most part, blokes hung on tenaciously to life without any pretence of bravery. What could be endured month after month, year after year, was amazing: battered and shrunken men struggled on with a little food, occasional repairs from doctors and support from mates. This triumph, both for those who survived and those who had the bad luck ultimately to succumb, deserves the highest respect and, for me, is the principal reason for perpetuating the memory of Far Eastern Prisoners of War.

Fourth, there is nothing remarkable about the spike in family breakdowns in the immediate post-war period either for POWs or returned servicemen generally. There were huge strains on families. What is truly remarkable is that the great majority of families held together through persistence, luck and bandaids of one sort or another, and have both the scars and fond memories to prove it.

Bibliography

Adam-Smith, Patsy (1992), *Prisoners of War: from Gallipoli to Korea*, Viking, Ringwood, Victoria.

Anon (1988), *Kanchanaburi: Spirit of the Death Railway and the River Kwai Bridge*, Indoor Design Company, Nonthaburi, Thailand.

Anderson, Karen (1981), *Wartime Women: sex roles, family relations and the status of women during the Second World War*, Greenwood Press, Westport, Connecticut, and London.

Atkinson, Les (2001), *My Side of the Kwai: Reminiscences of an Australian Prisoner of War of the Japanese*, Kangaroo Press, Sydney.

BBC, *WW2 People's War* (love in wartime, medical units, prisoner of war, Singapore 42, end of war, post-war years).

Beaumont, Jean, 'Prisoners of War in Australian National Memory', in Bob and Barbara Hately-Broad (2005), *Prisoners of War: Prisoners of Peace*, Berg, Oxford and London.

Blackater, C.F. (1948), *Gods without Reason*, Eyre and Spottiswoode, London.

Blainey, Geoffrey (2005), *A Short History of the Twentieth Century*, Viking, Melbourne, Victoria.

Blair, Joan and Clay (1980), *Return from the River Kwai*, Futura Publications, London.

Bowden, Tim (1984), *Changi Photographer: George Aspinall's Record of Captivity*, ABC Enterprises and William Collins Pty Ltd, Sydney.

Coates, Albert and Newman Rosenthal (1977), *The Albert Coates Story: The Will that Found the Way*, Hyland House, Melbourne, Victoria.

Cornelius, Mary (n.d.), *Changi*, Arthur H. Stockwell, Ilfracombe.

Costello, John (1985), *Love Sex and War: Changing Values 1939–45*, William Collins Sons and Co. Ltd, London.

Danaraj, T.J. (1990), *Japanese Invasion of Malaya and Singapore: memoirs of a doctor*, T.J. Danaraj, Kuala Lumpur.

Davies, Peter N. (1991), *The Man Behind the Bridge: Colonel Toosey and the River Kwai*, Athlone, London and Atlantic Heights, New Jersey.

Daws, Gavan, 1994, *Prisoners of the Japanese: POWs of World War II in the Pacific*, William Morrow and Company Inc, New York.

Dodkins, Marily (2006), *Goodnight Bobby: one family's war*, University of New South Wales Press, Sydney.

Donner, Wolf (1978), *The Five Faces of Thailand: An Economic Geography*, Queensland University Press, St Lucia, Queensland.

Dunlop, E.E. (1990), *The War Diaries of Weary Dunlop: Java and the Burma–Thailand Railway 1942–1945*, Viking Books, Ringwood, Victoria.

Durnford, John (1958), *Branch Line to Burma*, Macdonald and Co, London.

Ebury, Sue (1994), *Weary: The Life of Sir Edward Dunlop*, Viking, Ringwood, Victoria.

Feis, Hebert (1961), *Japan Subdued: The Atomic Bomb and the End of the War in the Pacific*, Princeton University Press, Princeton, New Jersey.

Flowers, Sibylla Jane, 'Captors and Captives on the Burma–Thailand Railway', in Bob Moore and Kent Fedorowich (1996), *Prisoners of War and their Captives in World War II*, Berg, Oxford and Washington DC.

Forbes, Cameron, 2005, *Hellfire: the story of Australia, Japan and the Prisoners of War*, Pan Macmillan, Sydney.

Gerson, Joseph (1995), *With Hiroshima Eyes: Atomic War, Nuclear Extortion and Moral Imagination*, New Society Publishers, Philadelphia and Gabriola Island, British Columbia.

Gruhl, Werner (2007), *Imperial Japan's World War Two 1931–1945*, Transaction Publishers, New Brunswick and London.

Guttman, Eric and Elsie Thomas (1946), *A Report on the Re-adjustment in Civil Life of Soldiers Discharged from the Army on account of Neurosis*, Ministry of Health, London.

Hardie, Elspeth (1983), *The Burma–Siam Railway: the secret diary of Dr Robert Hardie 1942–45*, Collins, Sydney and London.

Hartley, Jenny (ed) (1995), *Hearts Undefeated: women's writings in the second world war*, Virago Press, London.

Hately-Broad, Barbara, 'Coping in Britain and France: a comparison of family issues affecting the home coming of prisoners of war following World War II', in Moore, Bob and Barbara Hately-Broad (2005), *Prisoners of War: prisoners of peace*, Berg, Oxford and London.

Havers, R.P.W. (2003), *Re-assessing the Japanese Prisoner of War Experience: the Changi POW camp, Singapore, 1943–45*, RoutledgeCurzon, London and New York.

Hearder, Rosalind (2009), *Keep the Men Alive: Australian POW Doctors in Japanese Captivity*, Allen & Unwin, Crows Nest, New South Wales.

Holmes, Linda Goetz, 1993, *Four Thousand Bowls of Rice: a prisoner of war comes home*, Allen & Unwin, St Leonards, NSW, Australia.

Jeffrey, Betty (1997 edn), *White Coolies*, Angus & Robertson, Sydney.

Judt, Tony (2005), *A History of Europe Since 1945*, William Heinemann, London.

Kakizaki, Ichiro (2005), *Laying the Tracks: the Thai Economy and its Railways 1885–1935*, Kyoto University Press and Trans Pacific Press, Kyoto and Melbourne.

Kraatoska, Paul H. (ed) (2006), *The Thailand–Burma Railway 1942–46: Documents and Selected Writings*, Routledge, London and New York.

Lewin, Ronald, ed. (2007 edn), *Freedom's Battle Volume III: Voices from the War on Land 1939–1945*, Vintage Books, London.

Lomax, Eric (1996), *The Railway Man*, Vintage, London.

Lomax, Gina (2006), *Forged by War: Australians in Combat and Back Home*, Melbourne University Press, Melbourne.

Lumley, Joanna (1993), *Forces Sweethearts*, Bloomsbury, London.

Maynard, Roger (2009), *Hell's Heroes: The Forgotten Story of the Worst P.O.W. Camp in Japan*, HarperCollins Publishers, Sydney.

McKernon, Michael (2001), *The War Never Ends: the pain of separation and return*, Univeristy of Queensland Press, St Lucia.

McLaggan, Douglas (1995), *The Will to Survive: a private's view as a POW*, Kangaroo Press, Sydney.

Mills, Roy (1994), *Doctor's Diary and Memoirs: Pond's Party, F Force, Thai–Burma Railway*, RM Mills, New South Wales.

Moore, Bob and Barbara Hately-Broad (2005), *Prisoners of War: prisoners of peace*, Berg, Oxford and London.

Moran, Janet (1991), *Edwina Mountbatten: A Life of her Own*, HarperCollins, London.

Morrison, Ian (1943), *Malayan Postscript*, Angus and Robertson Ltd, Sydney and London.

Nelson, Hank (1985), *Prisoners of War: Australians under Nippon*, ABC Books, Sydney.

Nelson, Gordon (2005), *Men of the Line: Building the Burma–Thai Railway*, Australian Military History Publications, Loftus, New South Wales.

Newman, Carolyn (ed), (2005), *Legacies of our Fathers: World War Two prisoners of the Japanese – their sons and daughters tell their stories*, Thomas C. Lothian Pty, Melbourne, Victoria.

Parkin, Ray (1999), *Wartime Trilogy: Out of the Smoke, Into the Smother, the Sword and the Blossom*, Melbourne University Press, Carlton, Victoria.

Peek, Ian Denys (2003), *One Fourteenth of an Elephant: a memoir of life and death on the Burma–Thailand Railway*, Pan Macmillan Australia Pty Ltd, Sydney.

Perry, Roland (2010), *The Changi Brownlow*, Hachette, Australia.

Owen, Frank (1962), *The Fall of Singapore*, Pan Books Ltd, London.

Ramaer, R. (1994), *The Railways of Thailand*, White Lotus, Bangkok.

Reid, Pat and Maurice Michael (1984), *Prisoner of War*, Book Club Associates, London.

Richardson, Hal (1957), *One Man War: The Jock McLaren Story*, Angus and Robertson, Sydney and London.

Richards, Rowley (2005), *A Doctor's War Diary*, HarperCollins Publishers, Sydney.

Rimmer, P.J. (1971), *Transport in Thailand: the railway decision*, Research School of Pacific Studies, Australian National University, Canberra.

Rivett, Rohan, (1946), *Behind Bamboo: an inside story of the Japanese prison camps*, Angus and Robertson, Sydney and London.

Roberts, J.M. (1999), *Twentieth Century: The History of the World 1901 to 2000*, Viking, New York and London.

Rollings, Charles (2007), *Prisoner of War: Voices from Captivity during the Second World War*, Ebury Press, London.

Sanders, Kay, 'The World was Black: initial Australian reactions to the dropping of the atomic bomb on Hiroshima and Nagasaki', in Peter Dennis (ed) (1999), *1945: War and Peace in the Pacific*, Australian War Memorial, Canberra.

Silver, Lynette Ramsay (2004), *The Bridge at Parit Sulong: an investigation of mass murder: Malaya 1942*, The Watermark Press, Sydney.

Smith, Peter C. (1976), *The Battle of Midway*, New English Library, London.

Strategicus, (ND), *A Short History of the Second World War: and its social and political significance*, Faber and Faber, London.

Thamsook, Numnonda (1977), *Thailand and the Japanese Presence 1941–45*, Institute of South East Asian Studies, Singapore.

Tarling, Nicholas (2001), *A Sudden Rampage: The Japanese Occupation of South East Asia 1941–1945*, Hurst and Company, London.

The Yorkshire Post 1945–46.

Turton, Andrew (ed) (1978), *Thailand: Roots of Conflict,* Spokesman Books, Nottingham.

Walker, A.S. (1953), *Australians in the War of 1939–1945, Vol 2, Middle East and Far East*, Australian War Memorial, Canberra.

Waterford, Van (1994), *Prisoners of the Japanese in World War II: a statistical history, personal narratives and memorials concerning POWs in camps and on hellships, civilian internees, Asian slave labourers and others captured in the Pacific Theatre*, McFarland & Company Inc. Publishers, Jefferson, North Carolina, and London.

Webster, Donovan (2004), *The Burma Road: The Epic Story of the China–Burma–India Theater in World War II*, Perennial, New York.

Willmott, H.P. (2002). *When Men Lost Reason: reflections on war and society in the twentieth century*, Preager Publishers, Westport, Connecticut, and London

Wright, Joseph W. (1991), *The Balancing Act: a History of Modern Thailand*, Pacific Rim Press, Oakland, California.

Wright, Pattie (2008), *The Men of the Line: stories of the Thai–Burma railway survivors*, The Miegunyah Press, Melbourne.

Ziegler, Philip (2002), *Soldiers: Fighting Men's Lives 1901–2001*, Pimlico, London.

Index